GOLF

GOLF

building a solid game

Dr. Gary Wiren

Prentice-Hall, Inc., Englewood Cliffs, New Jersey   07632

Library of Congress Cataloging in Publication Data
Wiren, Gary.
   Golf: building a solid game.

   Bibliography
   Includes index.
   1. Golf. I. Title.
GV965.W72 1987   796.352'3   86-30544
ISBN 0-13-357948-4

Cover art: Steve Kuzma
Cover design: Wanda Labelska
Manufacturing buyer: Harry P. Baisley

Photographs appear on the following pages courtesy of the PGA of
America: 2, 7, 10, 13, 14, 97, 100, 102, 107, 119

Photographs appear on the following pages courtesy of Jeff McBride:
23, 26, 28-29, 34-40, 48, 50-55, 60, 81, 87, 104-105, 109-111, 112.

Printed in the United States of America

10 9 8 7 6 5 4 3 2 1

ISBN 0-13-357948-4   01

Prentice-Hall International (UK) Limited, *London*
Prentice-Hall of Australia Pty. Limited, *Sydney*
Prentice-Hall Canada Inc., *Toronto*
Prentice-Hall Hispanoamericana, S.A., *Mexico*
Prentice-Hall of India Private Limited, *New Delhi*
Prentice-Hall of Japan, Inc., *Tokyo*
Prentice-Hall of Southeast Asia Pte. Ltd., *Singapore*
Editora Prentice-Hall do Brasil, Ltda., *Rio de Janeiro*

To Ione, the rosy cheeked girl in the "Old G."

CONTENTS

7

THE SHORT GAME
where score can be influenced most quickly   **69**

8

RULES AND ETIQUETTE
golf's laws and manners   **79**

9

GETTING OUT TO PLAY
testing what you have learned   **91**

10

PRACTICE
the way to success   **98**

PREFACE

"Why do you want to learn the game of golf?" I've asked hundreds of beginners this question, and I've received answers such as: "Our company has an annual tournament and almost everyone else plays;" "I've watched it on T.V. and it looked interesting;" "My husband is a golf nut and I'm tired of staying home;" or simply, "It looks like fun." All of these answers have one thing in common. Each person is looking for satisfaction and enjoyment.

The first part of this book is addressed primarily to the elementary golfer. It assumes little or no golf experience on your part, so feel comfortable if you are a novice. The fresh treatment of golf's fundamentals, however, should provide a review for the more experienced player. In addition, the second portion of the book will take you well beyond the novice stage. In other words, this book may appeal to all levels of golfers.

If you become a golfer, you will be joining millions of other sportsmen and -women throughout the world who have found in this game a fascinating and enjoyable out-of-doors activity. The information contained in this book will help you reach that end and make your early experiences in golf more pleasant and rewarding.

1

GOLF

what to expect

Before you invest both time and effort,
this chapter will tell you:
1. What the game of golf expects of you.
2. What you may reasonably expect to receive in return.

Golf is a game and as such it is meant to be enjoyed. This is the first principle that the new golfer should understand. Golf can be a vivid test of your emotions and skills. But never let the test become so serious that you lose sight of the fact that enjoyment is your number one goal.

If you aren't sure what to expect from golf or whether you'll like it, just ask yourself the following questions. Do I have an active imagination? Do I have a desire to meet new people? Do I like to be out-of-doors in beautiful surroundings? (Figure 1–1) Do I relish a challenge? If you can answer "yes," then congratulations on your choice of activities—golf will serve you well. This chapter will discuss some of the personal requirements that you'll need to participate in golf successfully. It will also list some of the game's rewards and limitations. In order to judge the value of golf as an activity for you, you should formulate some questions about the game's positive and negative features.

PERSONAL NEEDS

A question certainly worth asking is, What personal qualities do I need to play golf? Assuming that you want to know those attributes possessed, in varying degrees, by the more than 20 million golfers in this country, here are the fundamental personal requirements.

1

Figure 1–1
The beauty of golf's surroundings helps make it a relaxing out-of-doors sport experience.

Motor Skill

Success in other sports is not necessarily an accurate predictor of your eventual success in golf. You needn't be a great athlete to enjoy golf. The "natural athletes" are sometimes discouraged because they are unable to master the game in a few sessions. On the other hand, the less physically adept persons who have to work hard for their results often accept the temporary failure as a natural step in learning. With continued practice their results are often better than those of their more talented counterparts. Naturally, the more physically talented and better coordinated you are, the greater initial potential you possess. But even our finest golf champions admit that desire and work are still two of the greatest attributes leading to success in the game.

Physiological

Golf is not designed to severely tax the human physiological makeup. People of all sizes and degrees of physiological composition have found satisfaction and success in the game. Most people require no special conditioning or training to play. This is not to say that good physical conditioning may not aid your performance—it certainly can—but simply to participate, that is, to walk nine or eighteen holes and hit your shots, does not normally require special physical conditioning. Some people might find it difficult to complete an eighteen-hole round of golf because they lack the stamina; but for most participants, the walk and mild exercise would prove to be more invigorating than taxing. If you possess greater than average strength and size, and at least normal flexibility, you may have an advantage over other golfers at your level. But golf equalizes some of the physical differences in individuals by requiring not only strength for good distance, but also accuracy and adeptness in the shorter strokes around the greens. In short, the physical requirements for enjoyable participation in golf are well balanced and certainly not overwhelming.

Psychological

The psychological qualities most necessary for enjoyable and successful participation in golf are patience, concentration, and a sensible approach to failure and success. You need patience to put in the necessary hours of practice even when you see little improvement. Concentration on the task at hand—swinging the club—is essential. Above all, you must have a good attitude toward early failures and problems; otherwise frustration can completely spoil the enjoyment of the experience as well as interfere with the learning process. Golf can be a source of relief from tension and stress, but it can also be a severe test of one's emotional control. Two emotions commonly displayed in the game are fear and anger. Your ability to cope with these two emotions will certainly affect your success and personal pleasure in golf.

The nervousness you may feel as you tee the first ball is caused by fear of not performing well—an emotion experienced by even the finest and seemingly most composed players. It can have devastating effects. Fear causes tension, and tension destroys the rhythm of the swing, which in turn can produce hosts of poor golf shots. If you experience this apprehension in your early games, it is usually only temporary and will diminish greatly when you begin to develop more confidence in your swing and in your ability. Tension will be further reduced when you fully understand that you are there on the course for enjoyment, and also when you put your results in the proper perspective.

Anger in golf, unless correctly channeled, is a self-defeating emotion. Golfers who can't control their anger leave the course with more tension than they had when they came. If you play so badly that you get angry enough to vow to do some practicing, then anger can be useful. But if your anger over a misplayed shot eliminates all pleasure in the game, you are defeating the initial purpose of being on the course—to have fun, to *play*. Thus, the "play-for-fun" golfer should possess enough self-discipline to control the tension that could result from fear or anger lest it spoil her or his recreation. If you have developed the ability to approach frustrating circumstances philosophically, then you needn't worry about one of the tougher psychological challenges of the game of golf.

GOLF'S REWARDS

Social Opportunities

Golf has a built-in system of socializing. Besides the sponsored golf activities that allow people to mix in any well-run golf club program, there is a universal tradition of pairing players who come to the course alone looking for a game. One man who has played at a local public links for thirteen years has never come to the course with a partner, yet he has always managed to find a game and has made hundreds of acquaintances through his golfing activity. Recently I was paired with a Houstonian visiting Canada, a man who has played golf in seventy-five countries, in every state capital of the United States, and in every British Commonwealth country (present or past) that has a course with the title "Royal" attached to its name. He travels almost exclusively alone but always finds a game. You may not be quite this adventuresome, but you can find many new friends through golf if you desire. Friendships made through golf can turn out to be some of the closest in your life.

Physical and Mental Conditioner

It should be obvious that the contribution golf can make to your physical fitness depends upon such factors as whether you ride or walk around the course, the speed at which you walk if you do, and whether you carry your own clubs.

Basically, an eighteen-hole round of golf on foot is equivalent to a four and one-half- or five-mile walk with intermittent stops. It is a moderate form of exercise having aerobic value that can leave you feeling exhilarated from being outdoors.

An equally important contribution toward health and well-being is the game's potential for relieving psychological tension. People have been introduced to the game by their physicians as a prescription for irritability and chronic fatigue caused by tension. Whether golf relieves tension is strictly dependent upon your personality and attitude toward the game. For some people with the wrong perspective on why they are there, a round of golf actually increases tension. In most cases, however, it is a valuable aid to relaxation, eagerly anticipated and enjoyed by millions.

Lifetime of Activity for All Ages

You may look forward to playing golf for a long time. John D. Rockefeller played regularly even after his ninetieth birthday, while an equally famous person, Arnold Palmer, began playing at the age of five. This wonderful age span makes the game an excellent family activity. One family in this country has an annual golf outing and putting championship at which they award a trophy. A surprise winner in one putting contest, the participants in which bridged four generations, was the eighty-four-year-old grandmother. Now that's a family sport! It's no wonder that golf has been called "the game of a lifetime."

Probably the greatest verbal tribute to golf and the best explanation of what you can expect from this game was given by D. R. Forgan:

> It is a science, the study of a lifetime, in which you may exhaust yourself but never your subject.
>
> It is a contest, a duel, or a melee, calling for courage, skill, strategy, and self-control.
>
> It is a test of temper, a trial of honour, a revealer of character.
>
> It affords a chance to play the man and act the gentleman.
>
> It means going into God's out-of-doors, getting close to nature, fresh air exercise, a sweeping away of the mental cobwebs, genuine recreation of the tired tissues.
>
> It is a cure for care—an antidote to worry.
>
> It includes companionship with friends, social intercourse, opportunity for courtesy, kindliness, and generosity to an opponent.
>
> It promotes not only physical health but moral force. (Forgan 1935, frontispiece)

IS GOLF THE RIGHT ANSWER?

Although golf has helped to fill the need for exercise and fun for millions of people in the world, it isn't the answer for everyone. Some have tried the game and quit; others have felt that golf wasn't what they wanted. Why?

Golf takes time—more time than many people have. Whereas you would consider two hours spent playing tennis, badminton, or handball to be a fairly complete workout, it takes the average American about twice that time to complete a round of golf—and longer in some metropolitan areas where the demand for golf facilities is great. In such cases it is not uncommon for a weekend golf outing (including time for getting to the course, waiting to get on the course, and playing) to stretch into an eight-hour ordeal. Man is finding an ever-increasing amount of leisure time available to him, but for some there's not yet enough time for golf. If time is a problem, consider that there are millions of nine-hole rounds of golf played annually in this country. A two-hour nine-hole round of golf is just right for many; plus, under the right conditions you can still find places where the three- to three and one-half-hour eighteen-hole round is played.

Golf costs money. When compared to skiing, boating, hunting, and some other activities, it is a relatively inexpensive activity; but for many budgets golf is out of reach. Greens fees, balls, and other minor accessories are ongoing expenses once the price of clubs, bag, and shoes has been met. If a person needs to make a choice depending heavily on

Figure 1-2
Golf cars are a big source of revenue but spoil one of the best reasons for playing the walk.

economy, he probably should be aware of some cost-saving ideas such as used rather than new equipment (both clubs and balls) and municipal courses where greens fees are modest.

Although golf is a great test of skill, it is not much of a test of physiological condition. A weekly game of eighteen holes is not enough exercise for a healthy person under retirement age. As a moderate form of activity, as mentioned, it is of worth to the otherwise sedentary individual; but golf alone as so many play it, in a golf car, is insufficient exercise to maintain a vigorous state of physical well-being. (Figure 1–2) If you play three to five times a week, hit practice balls, and walk during your rounds, that's a different story.

It is only fair that you realize from the beginning that golf, although a great game for many, can have some shortcomings and limitations. Try to steer clear of them. I hope you will find the game's liabilities not serious enough to prevent you from discovering its many assets.

AFTER READING THIS CHAPTER YOU SHOULD KNOW THAT:

The physical requirements to simply play the game of golf will not deter the "play-for-fun" participant.

Golf affords a psychological challenge that will test and/or help one learn to control one's emotions.

Golf is a social, recreational activity that can provide needed relaxation for people of all ages.

When compared with other individual sports, golf can be classified as moderately expensive and above average in time consumption.

Millions of golfers continue to find great enjoyment in their participation.

2

GOLF, THE GAME

then and now

In this chapter you will be introduced to:
1. Golf's origin, its development in the United States,
   and its effect on our culture.
2. The right attitude with which
   to face the game's challenges.
3. Basic features of the course,
   scorecard, and club design.

Golf has been called the Royal and Ancient Game—and deservedly so, for it can be traced to the fifteenth century when it was played by kings, queens, and noblemen. Records also indicate that university students at St. Andrews in Fife, Scotland, played it as early as 1415.

Games similar to golf were played earlier than the fifteenth century in Holland and France. A stick-and-ball game somewhat similar to golf, called "paganica," was played even at the time of the Roman Empire. But golf as we know it was popularized, if not invented, by the Scots.

EARLY GOLF IN THE UNITED STATES

Although records indicate that meetings of golfers were held in this country as early as the 1600s, the first officially established golf course in the United States that is still in existence must be credited to the town of Yonkers, New York. Built in the year 1888 and appropriately named the "St. Andrews Club," it was a crude three-hole, later six-hole, and finally nine-hole layout bearing a striking resemblance to a cow pasture—which it was. By 1900, twelve short years later, there were 1,000 courses in this country. Five U.S. Opens, five U.S. Amateurs for both men and women, and three intercollegiate championships had been held, and every state in the Union had a golf course. The game was definitely on its way.

Although facilities were being built at a startling rate, golf was still considered to be a "rich man's sport." The finest players of the early 1900s were well-to-do people with ample leisure time to practice and play. The average American considered golf to be a foreign game played by millionaires, and to a certain extent this was true. But in 1913, at the Country Club of Brookline, Massachusetts, an unheralded twenty-year-old local caddie named Francis Ouimet defeated the best players this country had to offer, plus the greatest golfers of the British Isles, Harry Vardon and Ted Ray. Ouimet thus became the first player born in this country to win the U.S. Open. With a new homebred champion, golf became an American game overnight.

CULTURAL CONSIDERATIONS

When a game is played by more than 20 million of the country's inhabitants, when these people spend more than a billion dollars annually on the game, when it captures several hours of network television programming a week, and when syndicated columns on the game are run in more than 100 of the country's leading newspapers—then that game indeed has some effect on the culture. In addition, golf is of particular interest from a cultural standpoint because it has nurtured an American institution called the "country club."

Not all golfers are country club members—far from it. Although more than 40 percent of the nation's courses are private, there are five times as many players who participate on public daily-fee courses. Many of the private club players were spawned on public courses, where they developed their golf interest to the point at which club membership was desired. For a family that wishes to play frequently, joining a reasonably priced club is sometimes a financial necessity.

The country club in some communities is a gathering place for families from several economic strata. In other instances it caters exclusively to the ultra-rich, and does not encourage family participation. Clubs determine membership in a variety of ways: social class, financial status, ethnic group, geographical location, religion, and place of business. Some country clubs represent the hedonistic, self-centered, prejudiced, bigoted aspects of our culture; others represent the genuinely healthy atmosphere of sport, family activity, fellowship, and fun, which might just be called a part of the "good life." In either case the country club, primarily because of golf, is a viable institution in our culture.

MENTAL ATTITUDE

If your approach to the game is to have fun, then you will have to learn occasionally to adopt a philosophical attitude toward your results. You won't *always* play well. One of the attractive qualities of golf, however, is

Figure 2–1
Even the stars who play for a living, such as Andy North, Jack Nicklaus, and Gary Player, find the companionship in the game great fun.

that you don't have to be a great player to enjoy it. You will soon discover that the average player with the right attitude has as much fun, or more, from his kind of game than does the highly skilled individual. The thrill that comes from breaking 100 for the first time is just as great for the amateur as is shooting a round below par for the expert. But don't think the experts don't have some fun too. (Figure 2–1)

You may become one of those rare people who learns to play the game near par, and you can derive much enjoyment from that accomplishment. But if you don't win the club championship or become the best player in your office or school, or even in your weekly foursome, don't despair. Though you may not capture headlines, look at it positively. You will get more shots for your money, exercise more, and see more scenic country than will your friends who play the low-scoring, long-hitting game down the middle. In the words of an early golfer:

> If the pleasure of golf lies in hitting the ball,
>   And in seven a hole you do,
> Then I, who have played fourteen in all,
>   Have had twice as much fun as you. (Sutphen 1901, p. 106)

That's the philosophical approach. But to be quite honest with you, the most fun in the game comes when you are improving.

THE CHALLENGE

No one can ever say that he has mastered the game of golf. Even the greatest players have been humbled by the game on many occasions. True, some phenomenal rounds of golf have been played in the game's history, but the perfect round has yet to take place.

At times you will feel that you have mastered the swing or some particular shot, and you may have—temporarily. But if you could collect ten cents for every time a golfer has said, "I finally figured it out; now I have it!" you would be very rich indeed. This *occasional* success is what makes the game a great challenge, for everyone can hit a shot like a professional—*sometimes*. Bobby Jones, the finest amateur player who ever lived, winner of the U.S. Open, U.S. Amateur, British Open, and British Amateur all in the same year (1930), succumbed to that feeling on at least one occasion. When still a youngster he came bolting into his father's study one day after having shot a 68 on the tough East Lake Country Club golf course, and announced that he never would shoot over 74 again. The following day he shot an 82! The diehard golfer lives on hope—hope for a better tomorrow—knowing full well that he can play better than he did today. There will always be the shot that shouldn't have strayed or the putt that could have dropped. Here lies golf's elemental fascination.

The game of golf is outwardly quite simple. You need only ad-

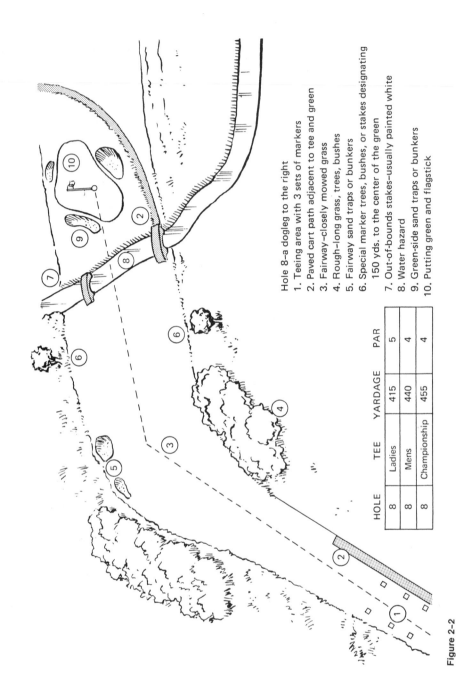

Hole 8–a dogleg to the right

1. Teeing area with 3 sets of markers
2. Paved cart path adjacent to tee and green
3. Fairway–closely mowed grass
4. Rough–long grass, trees, bushes
5. Fairway sand traps or bunkers
6. Special marker trees, bushes, or stakes designating 150 yds. to the center of the green
7. Out-of-bounds stakes–usually painted white
8. Water hazard
9. Green-side sand traps or bunkers
10. Putting green and flagstick

HOLE	TEE	YARDAGE	PAR
8	Ladies	415	5
8	Mens	440	4
8	Championship	455	4

Figure 2–2
The elements of a golf hole.

vance a small ball (1.68 inches in diameter) into a hole four and one-quarter inches in diameter in the least possible number of blows. You have a variety of tools (clubs) with which to accomplish this feat. Between the tee and the cup, however, a great deal can happen. The primary reason for unplanned and unwanted occurrences during a round is the nature of the facility on which you play—the golf course.

Figure 2–3A, B, C The challenges of the game can test the skills of even the finest players.

THE COURSE

It would be much easier to describe a tennis court, bowling alley, football field, or running track than a golf course since, with the exception of minor variations in materials and preparation, the former facilities are standardized. For golf courses there is no standardized layout. No two courses in the world truly play alike. Variety in the game's playing facilities is staggering. Adding to the challenges to one's imagination and skill is the factor of weather, which can markedly alter the playing conditions of a course in a matter of minutes. The better courses are carefully designed by a professional golf course architect who tries to shape the natural materials into an attractive and challenging test. Such a course is usually composed of the elements listed in Figure 2–2.

Some courses eliminate sand traps and rough in order to speed up play. Others seek to penalize the least errant shot severely by employing an abundance of traps, water hazards, and trees. (Figure 2–3 A, B, C) Like famous restaurants or unusual natural geographical sites, certain courses develop a worldwide acclaim that brings people to test and enjoy their unique contributions to the game. Names like Pine Valley, Pebble Beach, Augusta National, Muirfield, Winged Foot, Merion, and the "mecca," St. Andrews, all excite the avid golfer's imagination.

Finally, you will be impressed by the game's scenic beauty. Golf courses are located in some of the world's most beautiful settings. In places

Figure 2–4
The prospect of playing one of the fabled courses like Pebble Beach can quicken the heart of any avid golfer.

like Banff, the Monterey Peninsula, Hawaii, Hilton Head, and countless other breathtaking spots, you can be exposed to beauty that provides an aesthetic experience unsurpassed in other sports. (Figure 2–4)

THE SCORECARD

A golf scorecard (Figure 2–5) will be made available to you at the course when you go out to play. It contains basic information about the course and any local rules or conditions that you should know. Local rules pertain just to that particular course; for example, on a certain course in Florida, you are not required to play your ball when it comes to rest dangerously near an alligator. This type of information is usually located on the back of the card, possibly with a map of the course. On the inside of the card, you'll find the distance in yards from each set of tee markers to the hole. On some cards a graphic illustration of the hole is presented along with distances from easily identifiable landmarks.

Most holes run from just over 100 yards in length to just under 600 yards, with the occasional exception on either end. In addition to the standard-length eighteen-hole course of 6,000 to 7,000 yards for men, there are courses under 6,000 yards, known as "executive courses," and those even shorter called "par 3 courses." Par 3 courses have all short holes (usually under 250 yards) and are particularly recommended for beginning players. "Par," a term meaning the standard of excellence on a given hole, is based primarily on length (Table 2–1) and is indicative of the average score that an outstanding player would shoot on that hole with errorless play and two putts. The figures in Table 2–1 represent only recommendations, the final determination of par being a prerogative of the local course.

You'll also notice a column for handicap on the card. In order to equalize players of differing abilities, a national system of handicapping has been established by the U.S. Golf Association (USGA). The system is based upon the average of a fixed number of a player's best scores. It also takes into consideration the difficulty of the course upon which each score was made. The course's difficulty is expressed by its rating. A player who averages around 80 on a difficult course would probably have a handicap of 6, while a 2 handicapper would average about 75 or 76 strokes per round. If these two people were to compete in match play (a type of competition that decides a winner by the most number of holes won rather than the lowest total score), the 6 handicapper would receive 4 strokes. The handicap figure on the card indicates *where* he receives them. In this case (using the card in Figure 2–5), it would be on holes 5, 7, 14, and 18, the four most difficult holes. In a women's match with a difference of four in the handicaps, the strokes would fall on 7, 8, 13, and 16.

MEMBER CLUB U.S.G.A.   REPLACE DIVOTS / REPAIR BALL MARKS   COURSE RATING: MEN 71 72 WOMEN

HOLE	1	2	3	4	5	6	7	8	9	OUT	10	11	12	13	14	15	16	17	18	IN	TOTAL	HDCP	NET SCORE
CHAMPIONSHIP BLUE TEES	40_7	36_0	14_0	42_8	22_1	36_2	42_5	48_8	35_1	318_7	36_3	40_3	18_7	54_3	42_3	18_3	38_5	51_2	43_4	343_3	661_5		
MEN'S WHITE TEES	38_7	34_7	13_5	40_6	21_5	34_9	40_7	47_0	34_6	306_2	35_1	39_6	17_6	53_3	40_3	17_5	37_5	50_2	42_2	333_3	639_5		
MEN'S PAR	4	4	3	4	3	4	4	5	4	35	4	4	3	5	4	3	4	5	4	36	71		
MEN'S HDCP	5	13	17	7	3	11	1	15	9		18	6	12	10	2	16	8	14	4				
WON + LOST − HALVED 0																							
LADIES RED TEES	36_8	27_6	12_1	39_0	16_0	33_9	35_7	45_5	34_6	281_8	35_1	38_9	16_6	42_5	31_6	11_7	37_5	43_5	33_9	291_3	573_1		
LADIES PAR	5	4	3	5	3	4	4	5	4	37	4	5	3	5	4	3	4	5	4	37	74		
LADIES HDCP	7	15	17	5	13	9	3	1	11		14	6	12	2	10	18	4	8	16				

DATE _____   SCORER _____   ATTEST _____

Figure 2-5
A golf scorecard.

Table 2-1   Determination of Par

PAR	MEN	WOMEN
3	up to 250 yards	up to 210 yards
4	251 to 470	211 to 400
5	471 and over	401 to 575
6		576 and over

THE CLUBS

Golf clubs are simply tools of differing designs that are used to accomplish the task set before the player: to move the ball from one place to another. They are composed of a grip, a shaft, and a head, and are varied in design to solve the two problems that are common to the golfer: achieving the proper distance in the right direction.

A golf club is composed of the parts shown in Figure 2–6. The long-distance clubs are the woods. Because of their length, they can produce greater mechanical force than the other clubs. A standard-length driver for men is forty-three inches—four inches longer than the standard-length 2 iron. This added length makes the driver capable of moving the

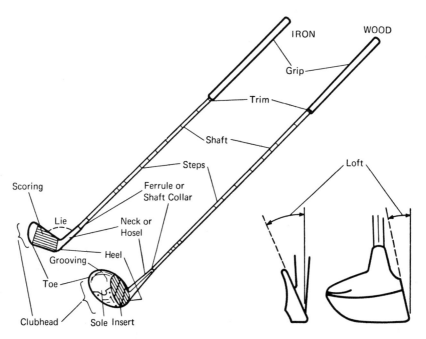

Figure 2-6
The parts of a golf club.

ball forty to fifty yards farther than the 2 iron for the medium-length-driving player. The irons are the accuracy clubs, to be used when you are close enough to reach the green. Their greater loft helps you control distance because it produces a high trajectory that causes the ball to stop soon after landing on the green.

The putter is an almost straight-faced club that is designed to roll the ball, rather than loft it, on the green. Putters come in a variety of styles; therefore, the only way you can intelligently select one is to try it out and see what success you have. It is not necessary to have the full complement of irons and woods to play the game.

After Reading This Chapter You Should Know That:

Golf as we know it became popular as early as the 1400s in Scotland but wasn't an established sport in this country until the late 1800s.

The sport of golf has since attained a high degree of popularity and influence in this country and has been largely responsible for the origin and perpetuation of the country club.

Each golf course is a unique sport facility designed to present the golfer with special problems while having a character all its own.

A scorecard contains information about local rules, par, yardage, course layout, and handicap stroke allocation. This information is helpful in informal play and essential in tournament competition.

Clubs are simply tools with which to play the game. They have gradual modifications in length and loft to afford the player a complete range of possible trajectories and distances within his own limitations.

3

EQUIPMENT

ideas on getting started

You now need the answers to some practical queries about:
1. *What equipment you need to play the game.*
2. *Whether you should rent or buy,*
   and how much you should pay.
3. *What brands and sizes are best.*
4. *What accessories you need.*
5. *How to care for the equipment once you have it.*

The equipment you use to play the game of golf can have an important effect on the degree of success that you achieve. Good equipment does not make a good golfer, but poor-quality or ill-fitting equipment can certainly hinder the performance of a player at any level of ability.

CLUBS

Rent or Purchase?

If you wish to play and do not own clubs, you may rent them for a nominal fee at almost any golf course pro shop. Rental equipment will suffice until you find out how serious you are about taking up the game. There are, however, several advantages to owning your own clubs. Each set has a particular feel to which you must become accustomed. Owning your own clubs provides you with the tools for practice and improvement. And having to rent or borrow equipment usually discourages one from regular play.

Where to Buy

Golf equipment is sold in a variety of stores, but usually the best place to purchase your equipment is in a golf professional's shop. These people know the merchandise better and usually stock higher-quality equipment than you will find in stores in which they also sell household appliances, automobile accessories, and other sporting goods equipment. At a golf shop you should also have the important advantage of trying the equipment on the driving range or on the course before you buy it. Golf shops will normally stand 100 percent behind their merchandise and replace faulty equipment within a reasonable length of time after the purchase, provided it has been used under normal conditions. Because they expect you to be a regular customer at their place of business, the golf course, they want you to have equipment with which you are satisfied.

What to Pay

Purchasing golf clubs need not be an expensive proposition. Although a full set of top-grade new clubs can run more than your budget will presently allow, there are less costly alternatives. One is a popular combination of clubs called a starter set consisting of 1 and 3 woods, 3, 5, 7, and 9 irons, and a putter. The price for a set of clubs of this kind—including a little bag to go with them—is modest compared with that for a full set. As you play more frequently, your judgment of distance will rapidly improve and you will find the need for additional clubs. Then it is wise to trade up to a better set rather than to fill in on those you already have.

You may feel that as a new golfer you cannot judge between quality and inferior clubs. However, the difference in performance and feel definitely exists. The discrepancy between top-grade and low-priced clubs might be described by saying that quality clubs are engineered while inferior ones are put together. The painstaking care that goes into making a top-grade club can be demonstrated by the fact that the finishing process alone on a top-quality wood club may take seven days to complete. Some difference in quality among different brands can even be found at the starter set level. The very cheapest sets are seldom good buys from either a performance or a durability standpoint. It is well worth the price to pay a few dollars more and invest in at least some degree of quality.

Often your best dollar value can be found in used top-grade equipment. Pro shops also have occasional close-out sales on new equipment at which they offer last year's top clubs at good discounts.

What Brands?

Particular brands are hard to recommend because the quality varies in the different price categories. The best golf equipment offered in complete lines from top grade to low price is usually made by one of the following manufacturers: Tommy Armour Golf Company, Spalding, MacGregor, Wilson, Ping, Hogan, Lynx, Powerbilt, Mizuno, Dunlop, and Ram. I don't generally recommend equipment specially made by or for wholesale houses, trading stamp concerns, or chain deparment stores. Although there are exceptions, much of this equipment is of an inferior quality or the training of the sales staff is inferior to that of the golf shop professional.

Fit

The experienced player will consider several factors when choosing his equipment: the club's length, its shaft flexibility or "whippiness," the swingweight or balance, grip size and material, head design, lie, and loft. Almost all players can find a proper fit in stock merchandise that does not require special manufacturing. You should be able to find a fit in clubs that are already in the pro shop or that can be ordered from the factory and received in a matter of a few weeks. Companies will usually offer in stock merchandise a choice of several features such as shafts, which are stiff for the long-hitting men, medium for the average male player, flexible for the softer-swinging men, and a ladies' shaft. You may generally choose between rubber or leather grips in either undersized, oversized, or regular circumference. Swingweight, which is a measure relating the weight of the clubhead to the shaft and grip, traditionally ranges from C0 to C9 for women and from D0 to D6 for men. In recent years, however, there has been a trend toward lighter clubs. The higher swingweight numbers and letters represent a heavier head feeling. Large golf manufacturing companies may offer several different designs or models from which to choose. They offer standard lofts and lies for their woods and irons, but custom specifications can be ordered for all aspects of the clubs.

Starter sets are made to fit the average player; that is, the clubs have a medium shaft, a regular length, and a regular grip size and are standard regular in all other dimensions. For a beginner or an infrequent player, these skeleton sets are usually adequate. If, however, you are among that group of people whose body type or level of strength differs markedly from the average, you might consider special-order clubs.

Here is one last bit of advice on club buying: Clubs are the single most important equipment item that you purchase in golf. Poor selection can severely hamper your enjoyment of the game. Get professional advice when you are contemplating the purchase of clubs. A top-priced set given to you as a gift is no bargain if it does not fit and you can't play decently with it.

OTHER EQUIPMENT

Shoes

Golf is still primarily a walking game. If your feet are uncomfortable, this can certainly lessen your enjoyment of the activity. Therefore, shoes become a vitally important piece of your equipment. Not only do they affect your comfort, but they also play an extremely important role in contributing to the effectiveness of your swing. You can play the game without golf shoes; however, you'll find it less comfortable and more difficult to obtain a solid base from which to swing.

For the majority of conditions in which you will play, a good pair of leather golf shoes that are properly maintained will prove to be the most comfortable and longest lasting of any currently on the market. New materials are continually being added to shoe lines, however, which may improve upon leather. Rubber waterproof shoes or golf rubbers are important to have in a wet climate or if you are an all-weather golfer. When purchasing shoes, expect to get strictly what you pay for in quality. Good shoes cost more money, but they are worth it.

Golf Bags

The type of golf bag you select will depend first of all upon whether you carry your clubs, ride a golf car, or use a golf pull cart. In some instances it is easier to carry your bag than it is to pull a cart, particularly when the course is extremely hilly. In addition, carts are rather cumbersome to get in and out of your car.

The lightest carry-type bags, called "Sunday bags," are made of canvas or vinyl. These bags are highly serviceable but generally do not have much storage space. Slightly larger carry bags do have extra compartments for storing golf accessories.

By the time you are a proficient enough golfer to own a full set of top-grade clubs, you might consider having two golf bags. One should be a large, durable bag with plenty of pockets for sweaters, rain gear, shoes, hand-warmer, golf gloves, tees, balls, ball markers, and an umbrella slip and the other a light carry bag. The large bag will probably be too heavy to carry around the course comfortably, but can be used with a pull cart or golf car. This kind of bag will come in very handy as a place to pack all your golfing equipment when you travel. (Figure 3–1)

Balls

You'll find a wide variety of golf balls from which to choose when you are ready to buy. There are currently three types of construction used in making balls: The conventional ball is made by winding bands of rubber around a core and placing a cover over the sphere; a two-piece and three-piece ball has synthetic material replacing the rubber bands; and a one-piece solid ball is made by injecting the ball's material into a preformed mold. Ironically, the wound ball replaced the solid ball on the market in 1902 because it would go much farther. With the introduction of new synthetics in the last two decades, it is now possible to make a solid ball that approximates the wound ball in performance. Since the solid ball is much simpler and less costly to make, it appears inevitable that history will reverse itself.

Figure 3-1
Get a nice light carry bag (such as the one I'm holding in the air) if you want to enjoy the walk in your round of golf. My Tommy Armour staff bag is for tournament play and exhibitions where I have a caddy, golf car, or cart.

Both solid and wound balls are made in varying compressions or degrees of hardness. Compression ratings range normally from 80 to 100, the higher figure representing the harder ball. Previously it was felt that it took a very strong person who was a hard swinger to effectively compress a ball rated at 100. It was recommended that a golfer of average length off the tee use a 90 compression ball, and a lighter swinger a ball in the 80 bracket. This theory has been challenged by research teams who contend that the high-compression ball will travel farther for all levels of players. This may be true; but an important consideration is feel, and the higher-compression ball generally feels too hard to the lighter-swinging player.

ACCESSORIES

Carts and Cars

Two types of club-conveying equipment are now in use: the pull cart and the powered golf car. If you do not own a light carry bag and find it difficult to carry your clubs for a full round, then a pull cart may be a necessary item for you. A good cart can be purchased in a wide range of prices, depending upon what accessories are included on it. Inexpensive carts are not very durable and are harder to pull than are the more expensive models. Pull carts may be rented at most public courses.

Electric and gasoline-powered golf cars have been a welcome addition to golf courses for the thousands of people who could not otherwise play. The presence of the powered car has brought many players back to the game who were forced to discontinue play because of physical infirmity. It has also induced many people to play golf who are unable to participate in other sports.

Unfortunately, however, powered golf cars are also being used by normal, healthy individuals who are sorely in need of some exercise. An increasing number of courses, anxious for additional revenues, are requiring that everyone who plays the course must take a golf car. At fifteen to twenty-five dollars per round rental, it is easy to see their financial viewpoint. This practice is definitely not in the best interests of the golfer who is being deprived of one of the game's more worthwhile attributes—the exercise. When you take "the walk" out of golf, you destroy one of its most valuable contributions to the participant. Never ride when you can walk.

Gloves

A golf glove aids in the firmness with which you can grip the club, and it also protects the hand from blistering. You may purchase either a full-fingered or a half-fingered glove. The full-fingered one is recommended. When you buy it, make certain that it fits snugly. The average glove, depending upon the quality of the leather, costs only a bit more than the price of a visor or golf cap and is a good investment.

Additional Items

1. When buying rainwear, be sure you are purchasing *waterproof* rather than rain-resistant or water-repellent equipment.

2. Tees come in different lengths. If you wish to have extra long tees, ask at the pro shop counter.

3. A telescoping ball retriever used for recovering balls from water hazards can pay for itself in a season if the course you play has several such hazards.

4. Golf clothing, as constrasted to street clothing, is especially designed for freedom of movement and comfort while playing.

5. Be cautious about the purchase of golf gimmicks or learning systems that advertise miraculous results. Some are helpful but get advice from your professional before buying.

MAINTENANCE TIPS

Protect your wood clubs by purchasing a set of head covers. Remove the covers during storage if they have gotten wet.

Clean your irons with soap and water, using a bristle brush. Never use abrasive cleaners or cleaning implements that might scratch a chrome finish.

Keep your rain gear neatly folded or on hangers when not in use to prevent the rubber lining from cracking.

Store your golf glove after each use in a plastic sack that you carry in your bag to keep the leather from drying and hardening.

Put a few drops of lubricating oil in the cleat housing of your golf spikes at the time of purchase and each time you replace cleats.

Wax your wood clubheads occasionally with furniture wax.

Leather grips may be washed to maintain their "tackiness." Avoid the use of solvents.

AFTER READING THIS CHAPTER YOU SHOULD KNOW THAT:

Having your own golf clubs is an advantage because it encourages you to play more frequently and gives you a consistent feel in their use from one outing to the next.

A starter set, or half set, consists of the odd-numbered clubs in the bag plus the putter, and is a sufficient selection at the beginning.

The majority of players can be "fit" with clubs from standard stock items. If *you* can't, then consider grip size, shaft length and flexibility, weight, materials in the grip, shaft, and head, design, loft, and lie when ordering.

Because golf is primarily a walking game, shoes are an important item in selecting equipment.

Higher-compression or harder balls will travel farther for all golfers, but may not be practical for some players because of feel.

A golf glove will both protect your hand and give you a better gripping surface.

4

GRIP AND STANCE

the preliminaries to the swing

As you prepare to make the swing,
you will learn the importance of:
1. Aiming the clubface.
2. Different styles of gripping the club.
3. Body posture, alignment, and ball position.

Having become acquainted with the game of golf and its equipment in the first chapters, you must now investigate the mechanics that are needed to develop a sound technique and style of play.

There are two distinct phases to making a successful golf shot. The first phase is passive and involves your preparations to swing; it will be discussed in this chapter. The second phase is active and involves performing the swing itself and striking the ball. This more dynamic phase will be dealt with in Chapters 5 and 6.

BEFORE YOU SWING

The fundamental preparations before the swing that go into making a good golf shot could well be labeled the "unappreciated necessities." Just as viewing a successful rocket launch is much more exciting than studying the detailed planning that put the capsule into space, so swinging, rather than preparing to swing, seems to capture the interest of the amateur golfer. Though the blast-off or swing may be sound, without the proper preliminaries the result could be failure. A golf stroke has a better chance of succeeding with good preparations and a mediocre swing than it does with inadequate preliminaries and a sound swing.

CLUBFACE ALIGNMENT

Golf is a target game using a ball as the object with which to hit that target. If you want to drive a ball in any sport toward a given spot, you must present the striking surface of your bat, club, paddle, hand, or whatever at right angles to your intended line of flight.

In golf the striking surface is the clubface. If the ball rebounds to the right of your target, the face (in golf terminology) has been presented "open"; if the ball goes to the left, it has come in "closed." To learn to hit the ball straight consistently, you must be able to repeatedly deliver your clubhead swinging on a path toward the target and return the face squarely to the ball. You can check to see that you are starting the clubface in that position by a simple exercise.

Using three clubs, make a simulated letter "H" as illustrated in Figure 4–1. Club A will point to the target and will be called the *target line*. Club B represents the *foot line* upon which the toes of each foot will be placed when assuming a square stance. Club C at right angles to the

Figure 4–1
Place two clubs parallel on the ground. Point the one farthest from you just to the right of your target so that a similar starting line running through your ball will point to your target. The closer club is for your foot alignment, helping set your body parallel to the flight line. The third club is to aid in determining ball position.

Figure 4-2
The third club placed on the ground to identify ball position should be set at right angles to the others. Note the ball is played slightly left of center, as you face the ball, some three to four inches inside from the left heel.

Figure 4-3
Check to see the clubface is square by soleing it on the flight line club.

Figure 4–4
Also check your shoulder alignment by placing a club across your shoulders. It should point parallel left of your target.

Figure 4–5
To further help you check your body alignment place a club across your thighs to check hip alignment. It should be parallel to your target line and left of the target.

others is called the *ball line* and indicates the position of the ball relative to your feet. (Figure 4–2) Now, stand comfortably so that your toes are almost parallel to the foot line. Take your grip with a 5 or 7 iron, and sole the club on your target line. (Figure 4–3) When the leading edge of your iron makes a right angle to line A, you are soling the club with a squared face. Let the grip end of your club point to your left hip when practicing this exercise. Spend some time in your first few practice sessions checking this so that you become accustomed to seeing the correct club positioning. This is important, for when you actually play, the ball is resting in the grass and you are not allowed artificial alignment devices. You may also check your body alignment by setting a club across your shoulders (Figure 4–4) and hips. (Figure 4–5)

POSITIONING THE HANDS

Now that you can sole the club properly, you are ready to position your hands on the grip portion of the club. This is referred to in most golf circles as "taking your grip," or just "gripping." Many people mistakenly interpret that term as "squeezing," the kind of squeezing you see applied to grip-strength machines in penny arcades. You don't want to hold a golf club with that type of "grip." When we refer to a grip, think more of positioning the hands than of squeezing the club.

Importance of Grip

Probably the most important aspect of any successfully run operation is its *communications* system. When communication stops, is faulty, or is inaccurate, look for problems. The only link of communication that you have with the golf club is your hands. Proper hand positioning, then, becomes a vital key in the whole process of a golf shot. It is extremely important to develop a good grip immediately so that your line of communications is correctly established. Find a fundamentally sound position at the beginning, and stick with it!

Positioning the left hand. Stand with your feet at shoulder width, and sole the club (a 5 or 7 iron). Rest the clubhead approximately four inches inside the left heel toward the middle of your stance. Straighten out your left arm so that it is comfortably extended, palm open; and then align the shaft and grip of the club with your arm, which should make an almost continuous straight line from your left shoulder to the clubhead. Now, cock the wrist downward until you can place the grip of the club at a slight diagonal across the fingers coming out under the heel pad of the palm. (Figure 4–6A)

Close your fingers around the club and elevate your arm, keeping

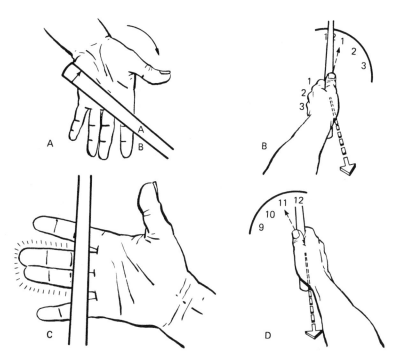

Figure 4-6
Positioning the hands. (A and B) Left-hand grip. (C and D) Right-hand grip.

the whole unit of arm and club straight, until the clubhead is a foot or two in the air. You should feel the pressure of the club's weight under the heel pad of your hand. In this position you should also be able to see the first two or three knuckles on the back of your left hand. If you can't, sole the club and rotate your hand in clockwise movement until you can see two or three knuckles. Whether you should have two or three knuckles visible will be discussed later in the chapter. Repeatedly raise and lower your arm and club this way until you feel security in your hold on the club, particularly in the last three fingers.

Now place your left thumb against the portion of your hand below your index finger so that they make a web. This web will form an inverted "V" that points somewhere between your chin and right shoulder. (Figure 4–6B) Rest the thumb and index finger on the grip so that the club is carried in the channel made by joints A and B of the finger and so that your thumb points to a position approximating one o'clock on an imaginary clock face. The club in your left hand should be a combination finger-and-palm grip.

Positioning the right hand.   Place the club so that the grip runs diagonally across a point near the base of the fingers. Close your fingers around the club, placing primary gripping emphasis upon the ring and middle fingers in the right hand. (Figure 4–6C) Now make a web between your thumb and the base of your index finger, so that the apex of the "V" formed by the web points just to the right of your chin. (Figure 4–6D) Cock your wrist slightly downward, and the natural hollow in your right hand should comfortably cover your left thumb already on the grip. Now place the thumb of the right hand at an eleven o'clock position, a little on the left side of the shaft. Even more than the left hand, the *fingers* of the right, rather than any part of the palm, should be conscious of controlling the club. Think of holding the club more like a pencil than a hammer.

You now have what is known as a full-fingered grip (sometimes erroneously called a "baseball grip"). In other words, all fingers are in contact with the club. Although some successful touring professionals use this method, it is not the grip practiced by 90 percent of the best players in this country. There is one more step to perform before you assume the most popular grip position. What you decide upon with regard to final hand position, however, should be a choice made by you and your instructor relative to your own physical traits.

Three Types of Grips

The overlapping grip, named after the great English champion of the early 1900s, Harry Vardon, who popularized the technique, has won by far the widest acceptance of all the golf grips. But individual differences will dictate that one grip may not be the answer for everyone. The goal of sound hand positioning is to provide a balance of power between the two hands while maintaining control and feel. In right-handed players, the dominant right is usually much stronger. To balance the strengths of the two hands and also to evolve a better coupling, the overlapping and interlocking positions were devised. Look at the illustrations and descriptions of the styles in Figure 4–7, and check the accompanying chart to help you decide which method suits you. Some experimentation may be necessary; but with the help of a teacher or professional, settle on one method soon and stick with it.

Grip Pressure

How much gripping pressure do you exert to position your hands properly? We sometimes hear the words "firmly" and "lightly" used in reference to grip, but these terms are only relative. What is firm to a person with weak hands may be light to another with strong hands. The best way to test for the correct amount of grip pressure is to ask these questions:

Descriptions of Three Grip Styles
(Club held vertically wih the clubhead in the air)

Overlapping	Interlocking	Full Finger
Slide your right hand down the grip until your little finger rests in the notch made by the middle finger and the slightly triggered index finger of your left hand. Your little finger does not have to hook clear around the knuckle. 	Remove the index finger of your left hand and, moving your right hand slightly down the grip, lace the two fingers together. Maintain your right-hand grip primarily in the fingers. 	Explained in the text. All fingers on the grip. 

Criteria for Selection

	Overlapping	Interlocking	Full Finger
Finger and hand size . . .	Normal to large	Small hands, thick fingers	Usually smaller hands
Strength . . .	Normal to strong	Normal to strong	Usually weaker
Hand balance . . .	Strong right dominance	Right dominance	Less dominant right
Est. % of use* . . .	63%	25%	10%

*Approximately 2% use some other grip.

Figure 4–7
Hand positioning.

Too firmly?

Is the blood being squeezed from my fingers?
Are my forearms tight?
Do I have little wrist suppleness?
Am I unable to sense the weight of the clubhead when I swing?
Does the club feel like a long stiff stick?
If the answer to any of these questions is "yes," you are probably gripping the club too tightly, usually in the right hand.

ADDRESS POSITIONS

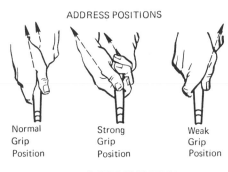

Normal
Grip
Position

Strong
Grip
Position

Weak
Grip
Position

PROBABLE IMPACT POSITIONS

Square Face

Closed Face

Open Face

Figure 4-8
Three grip positions and their influence on the clubface at impact.

Too lightly?

Does the club turn in my left hand when I hit the ball?

Is there daylight showing between my fingers and the grip?

Does the club bounce at the top of my backswing?

Is there a hole or space formed at the base of my left little finger, which comes from not having my little finger securely encircling the grip?

If you can answer "yes" to any of these questions, you are probably gripping too loosely, particularly in your left hand.

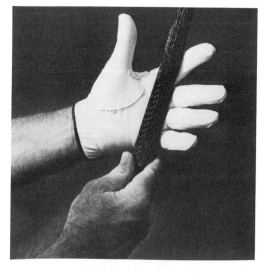

Figure 4-9
Lay the club at a slight diagonal across the base of your fingers in the left hand.

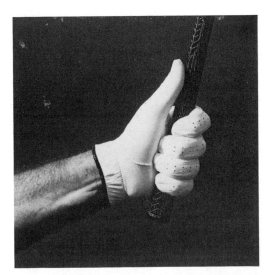

Figure 4-10
When you close your left hand you will feel the club securely captured by the last three fingers of your left hand.

Strong or weak position. It would be foolish to assume that everyone should grip the club in exactly the same way. It is both impossible and impractical—impossible because hands come in a great variety of sizes and shapes, and impractical because hands vary in strength and flexibility.

The number of knuckles to see and the place where the "V" from the web between the thumb and index finger points are two mechanics to be decided after you have hit some balls. The most natural and sensible position is one in which your arms are hanging comfortably and need only to swing into a position where your fingers may encircle the grip. But

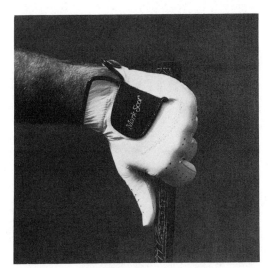

Figure 4-11
Place your left hand on the grip so that a small portion of the butt of the club is visible from this position. Never grip over the end of the club.

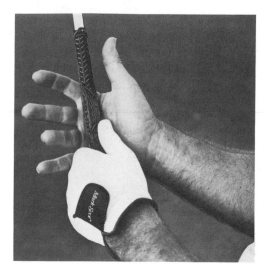

Figure 4-12
Do not place the club deep in your right palm.

Figure 4-13
It will end up looking like this, as though you are grasping a hammer ready to hit.

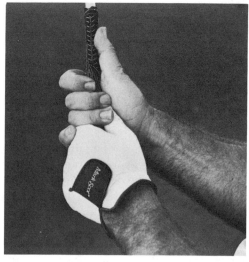

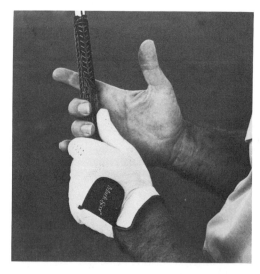

Figure 4-14
Instead place it in the fingers so that the primary grippers are your right and middle fingers.

36

Figure 4-15
It will then look like this, ready to swing.

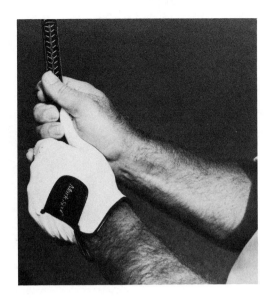

Figure 4-16
This is the all-finger grip where no fingers are laced together or overlap one another. It is used most often by people whose hands are small or not strong.

Figure 4-17
This is the interlocking grip where the index finger of the left hand and little finger of the right hand are laced together. Be careful not to lace them so deeply that the right grip goes from being carried in the fingers to the palm.

Figure 4-18
This is the overlapping grip where the little finger of the right hand laps over the index finger of the left hand, either lying on top of it or lying in the groove between the middle finger and the index finger. This is the most widely used grip in golf.

slight adjustments may be necessary and can be found only by experimenting. Apply the fundamentals about gripping that you have learned, and then adjust the position of your hands until you are hitting the ball straight. The adjustments and their effect on the clubface at impact are shown in Figure 4-8. Something very close to the "normal" grip position is where you should end up. Take great care in developing your grip, and frequently consult with your teacher about your progress. Above all, be patient and particular. A good grip is an invaluable asset to your development as a golfer. Now check the illustrations Figure 4-9 to 4-18 to make sure you have it correct.

STANCE AND ADDRESS

Once you have determined the grip you plan to use, aligned the clubface, and carefully placed your hands on the grip, you must prepare to address the ball. There is an athletic, at-ready position known as "stance" that is common to many sports, including golf. With only slight changes of body attitude, you'll find that shortstops, quarterbacks, defensive basketball players, tennis players, and many other athletes prepare for action by spreading their feet to shoulder width, flexing their knees, and bending slightly forward at the waist. Making these adjustments from the upright carriage position gives one a solid base from which to move, lowers the center of gravity, and improves equilibrium.

This position can also be adapted to golf. With both hands placed on the grip—while the shaft is fixed in a continuous line with the left arm—elevate the club in front of you. Gradually bring your arms and the club down until with the left arm you feel slight pressure on the chest. (Figure 4–19) Bend forward at the hips to a point where the club is touching the top of the grass. (Figure 4–20) Finally, flex your knees slightly, just enough to sole the club properly. (Figure 4–21)

      This technique will help you find the correct distance to stand from the ball for all your clubs while taking into consideration your body build. Tall, lean people will end up standing closer to the ball than heavy-set types. But in any case you should feel your arms hanging rather than reaching—hanging in an extended rather than a limp position. The flexing of the knees gives your swing the cushion that allows you to turn on the power without losing your fluid motion.

Feet and Weight

Finding the correct position for your feet and weight is a simple matter; more than likely you will do it intuitively. The feet are spread to about shoulder width to stabilize balance. Men have a tendency to spread their feet wider than women in order to hit the ball harder. Actually, great spread often decreases distance since too much space between the feet inhibits

Figure 4–19
Finding the correct distance from the ball is determined by:
(1) Bringing your arms down until you feel pressure on your chest.

Figure 4-20
(2) Bending forward at the hips, soleing the clubhead with the arms hanging extended.

Figure 4-21
(3) Adjusting your feet to their proper width and alignment. The arms are now neither crowded nor reaching.

the turning of the hips and shoulders, a move essential to power. Female players will frequently stand with their feet too close together and therefore lack adequate balance to wind up and take a full cut.

There are two directions in which to balance your weight: forward-backward and laterally. You can maintain the best forward-backward balance by distributing weight between the balls and heels of your feet—never on the toes or heels alone. Your lateral balance will vary somewhat with the club you are using. The weight at address tends to favor the left side on a short-iron pitch swing (about 60 percent left to 40 percent right), but equalizes more as the stance becomes wider and can become 60 percent right and 40 percent left when you reach the driver. On all swings the weight that is on the right foot at address should exert some pressure on the inside of that foot, so that the right leg may better resist too much lateral movement to the right and be able to push toward the left during the swing. Bracing your right knee inward at address will help you achieve this position.

Your feet should be arranged so that the back foot points on a line almost at right angles to your target. The left foot will be turned ten to twenty degrees out from this line toward the target. (Figure 4–22) Turning the left foot out will help you clear the left side so that you are able to complete the hitting action all the way through the shot. If a line were drawn from the right toe through the left toe in your regular stance, it should run parallel to your line of flight; this is known as a "square stance." The open and closed stances are variations that are used for specific types of shots, which you'll see later. Notice that your stance also can influence the line on which you swing and therefore affect the flight of the ball.

Ball Placement

Two theories on ball placement with relation to your feet are common. One would have you assume a different relationship for ball and feet for every single club. The other, the one that will be demonstrated here, keeps the ball in a constant position relative to your left foot on all irons and makes slight changes for the woods. In the constant-positioning method, the ball for all iron shots is placed between three and four inches toward the center of the stance from a line inside the left heel. The only variable is the right foot, which controls the width of the stance and the center line of your body. The width of your stance will decrease as the shot becomes shorter. (Figure 4–23)

In the wood clubs played from the grass (fairway woods), move the ball one to two inches farther toward your left foot. The driver, since it is hit from a tee, can be played even farther forward in your stance. Place it just in back of a line from your left heel or instep. You will acquire slight variations in these positions as you develop your own style of play.

Probable swing line related to stance
"On target"

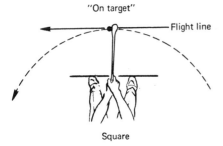

Square

Probable swing line related to stance
"Outside-in"

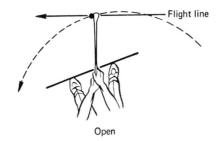

Open

Probable swing line related to stance
"Inside-out"

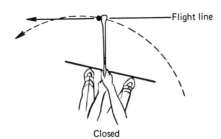

Closed

Figure 4-22
How stance can influence swing line.

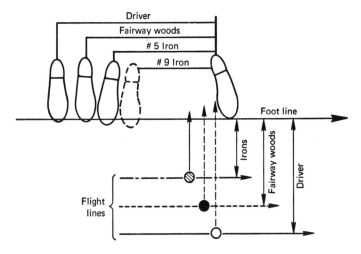

Figure 4-23
Relationship of ball to feet in the stance.

The most important considerations in stance and ball placement are:

1. Stand comfortably, weight favoring your left side more on the shorter shots, balancing on the medium shots, and favoring the right slightly on tee balls (driver).

2. Keep the ball placed far enough forward from the middle of your stance so that you don't have to "reach back" to hit it.

3. Stand so you are neither crowding the ball nor reaching out for it.

Developing a Routine

The more consistent you can become in making these preparations before you swing, the greater are your chances for success. Therefore, try to develop a routine that you follow automatically in the course of getting ready to hit a golf shot.

1. Select your club and feel how strongly you intend to swing it.

2. Approach your shot from behind your line to the pin so you can visualize where you want to aim.

3. Take a careful and uniform grip.

4. Sole the clubhead behind the ball while measuring off with your left arm or chest the correct distance to stand from the ball. Place the bottom line of the clubface at a right angle to your line of flight.

5. Draw an imaginary line, perpendicular to your line of flight, which runs from the clubhead to the correct position between your feet for the placement of the ball for that particular club.

6. Place first your right foot, then your left, into a position that is comfortable and correct for that club, and keep the clubface square to the target.

7. Make your swing.

The practice of a brief but systematic routine such as this, which incorporates the essential preliminary preparations, will bring you closer to the essence of good golf—consistency.

YOUR PRACTICE SHOULD BEGIN WITH THE REALIZATION THAT:

Many golf shots are "spoiled" before the swing ever starts because of faulty preparation. In fact, most swinging errors stem from an incorrect grip, stance, or alignment.

The clubface is "square" to the target when its bottom edge is aligned at right angles to the intended line of flight.

Your hands are positioned squarely to the target or near that position when the back of your left hand and the palm of your right hand face it.

Because of individual differences, all players will not grip the club in exactly the same manner.

The correct golf stance will find the player with his arms in an extended hanging position, the feet comfortably spread, the right knee braced inward, the weight balanced between the balls and heels of the feet, and the ball placed forward of the center of the stance, farther ahead for woods than for irons.

You should develop a definite routine in your advance preparations that allows you consistently to find the correct grip, stance, and address on all your shots.

5

THE GOLF SWING

a feeling to be developed

You are now ready to learn how to:
1. Identify the important principles of the swing.
2. Fit them to your abilities and body type.

One of the facts that golf's greatest players agree upon is that legendary PGA professional Sam Snead had a "classic swing." It was a picture of flowing but powerful rhythm culminating in a sweep of the club through the ball that excluded the slightest hint of forced effort. It was reminiscent of a perfectly executed swan dive from five meters—never a hurried move, never a loss of control. Contrast that to the lashing swing of Lanny Wadkins, the laconic lightness of Jerry Pate, the mechanical precision of Tom Watson, and the abbreviated but powerful swat of Dan Pohl—all touring professionals. Then tell me which swing is best. Well, Snead's was best—that is, for Snead. And probably it would also be the best swing style for most novice golfers to emulate. True, it may not work for Wadkins or Watson or the others because they may be physically constructed to swing in another way. You may not be able to swing like Sam Snead either, but the closer you get to that rhythm and sequence, within your own limitations, the better you'll play.

All of these players have developed a personalized style that has become successful for them only after countless hours of experimentation and practice. For the most part, they swing the golf club quite well, but some of their swinging habits should *not* be copied! Obvious physical differences and limitations will tell you that if you are six feet, five inches, 175 pounds or five feet, nine inches, 200 pounds, you won't be able to swing just like five-foot, nine-inch, 165-pound Tom Kite no matter how hard you try. More subtle discrepancies between you and a PGA tour star may exist in strength, flexibility, and even in temperament, which will dictate a necessary difference in style. So as you start your golf swing education, recognize that individual differences among successful players exist. Then consider the following suggestions:

1. Most instructional books written by professionals are "How I Do It" books, or personal testimonies of the techniques that each particular pro uses.

2. Be aware that what works wonders for Watson may not be the answer for you.

3. With so much varied expert opinion available, select one system and stay with it. Building an effective swing by using a little of the best from several contrasting methods is at best improbable.

4. In choosing whom to emulate in your swing, select a player who resembles you in body type and, if possible, in temperament.

THEORY OF THE SWING

Now that you are aware that certain differences exist in the swings of fine players, let's see in which ways their swings are alike. In searching for the similarities of the swings of successful players, try to discard the mannerisms that needn't be copied, and focus your attention on the principles that make their swings work. Any golf swing must have these essentials: clubhead speed, accuracy, and consistency or repeatability. If any of these three items is lacking, it is impossible to become a good player from the standpoint of striking the ball.

In order to blend these three characteristics into a movement called a golf swing, the following principles are employed by the fine players:

1. The club is swung in a nearly circular fashion around the player, away from and then toward the target.

2. The center or hub of that swing is located in the middle of the player's neck or chest.

3. The wrists hinge, providing a second lever in the swing, which generates additional force.

4. As the swing approaches impact, angular momentum travels from the center of the swing out to the clubhead, slowing the arms down and speeding the clubhead up. This force allows the clubface to square itself to the target without added manipulation of the hands.

5. The focus should be on swinging the club *through* to a balanced finish rather than hitting *at* the ball.

Though these principles mean little to you at the moment because they are simply words, it is important to become acquainted with them. As you begin to convert your mental perception of the swing into action, you can come back to them again to see if you are on the right track.

FEELING A SWING

There are two approaches to striking a golf ball—swinging and hitting. The swinging style of a Sam Snead is what will be advocated in this book because it follows exactly the principles that we have just discussed. To develop consistency in a hard-hitting swing like Arnold Palmer's takes years of practice and the hitting of thousands of practice balls. In addition, it requires a great deal of playing and practice to maintain the timing for successful repetition.

On the other hand, a swinging hit, like Snead's, demands less from the golf student and does not require as much practice to maintain. When we talk of swinging, we will be considering a smooth-flowing action with gradual acceleration that allows the player to feel centrifugal force through the clubhead.

DEVELOPING A SWING

Footwork

In any striking or throwing motion in which you are trying to generate speed, the transfer of weight and the development of power that comes from trunk rotation are important. To develop these features, you must establish a fundamental known as "footwork." Your first physical introduction to the golf swing in this book will be to take a part of the swing— footwork—and develop it in conjunction with an arm swing.

Place a club on the ground representing your target line. Then stand with your feet at shoulder width, your arms hanging in front of you. Bend forward at the waist and flex your knees slightly, assuming a position similar to your correct golf posture. (Figure 5–1A) Now imagine you are a wheel, a large wagon wheel: Your arms are the spokes, and your head is the hub. Start your arms swinging by rotating your trunk and shoulders to the right, letting your arms follow in that direction. (Figure 5–1B) Then reverse the direction to the left to unwind the wheel. Your arms will return to their starting position initiated by a weight shift to the left. Gradually increase the turning until your chin is meeting your left shoulder on the backswing and your right shoulder on the follow-through. This should be done in such a way that your head moves very little during the swing except to rotate slightly to the right on the backswing and to the left and

Figure 5-1A DRILL #1 ARMS HANGING. Place a club on the ground pointing to your target. Hang your arms in front, right hand below left, and align them on the shaft of the club. All your swings will see your hands come from inside the club line, onto the shaft going toward the grip then back to the inside again.

Figure 5-1B Swing your arms back so as to wind your upper body over your right leg. Get your back to face the target. Your left heel may rise slightly and your left knee will flex inward.

Figure 5-1C Swing through a position similar to address except now the weight is a bit more on the left foot and there is a bit more sit in your knees. The back of the left hand and right palm face the target in the impact position. This is critical.

Figure 5-1D Finish completely on the left side, comfortably erect with the right heel in the air and pointing directly back away from the target.

finally up on the follow-through. Your arms should be hanging separately and extended.

Observe the accompanying footwork resulting from the correct performance of this winding and unwinding as pictured. On the backswing you will feel a desire to raise your left heel in the air as you complete the full windup of your arms and shoulders. This is correct in a full-motion swing for a long shot. But if the heel is elevated more than a couple of inches, it is a warning sign indicating that your head is probably moving laterally too far to the right and also upward. Keep your head a bit more still so that your arms rotate around it in a *turning*, not a lifting, action. The heel will then stay closer to the ground.

The most important part of your footwork comes after you have reached the top of your backswing. At that point, reverse the direction of your swing motion by first getting your left heel down solidly on the ground by transferring your weight more to your left leg. This is done in a fashion similar to throwing a ball in a side-arm fashion. Roll off the inside of your right foot, while your hips are moving laterally and rotating to the left. Let your right hand and the back of your left hand face the target at the impact position. (Figure 5–1C) At the finish of this motion, your belt buckle should make a ninety-degree turn from its original facing-the-ball position to one facing the target. And your weight will be almost completely on the *outside* of your left foot. (Figure 5–1D)

You must practice these fundamentals without a club until they become automatic, first with both arms swinging (Drill #1), then with the left arm alone (Drill #2: Figure 5–2A, B, C, and D); then again use the left arm but now with three fingers of the right gripping the left thumb (Drill #3: Figure 5–3A, B, C, D) and continuing through Figures 5–4, 5–5, 5–6, and 5–7. This series of drills will beautifully prepare you for the next step, placing an object, the ball, in the way of your swing. Unless you have mastered these elementary positions it is a waste of time to try to hit practice balls, let alone play. In a few practice sessions of five to ten minutes, you can acquire the necessary basic skills. (Figure 5–8)

When you do these drills pay attention to the following points:

1. Make a full shoulder turn on the backswing so that you literally "wind up" and have your back facing the target.

2. Keep your head reasonably well centered so that you can learn to return to a position where you'll consistently make contact with the ball.

3. Practice all your swings so that your hands come from inside to down the line, feeling slightly outside of that line, then back to inside of the club placed on the ground.

4. Always get your weight to your left side in the swing.

5. Have your wrist cocked but flat, with your forearm at the top of the swing. Release the cocking on the downswing so that you hear a "whooshing" sound when swinging the club and the back of your left hand faces the target at impact.

Figure 5-2A DRILL #2 LEFT ARM ALONE. Make a fist with your left hand and point your extended thumb above the club shaft. Place your right hand behind your back.

Figure 5-2B Wind to the top of your swing so the left thumb points parallel to the target line. Keep your left hand closed and wrist flat.

Figure 5-2C Back of the left hand facing the target at impact.

Figure 5-2D Finish again completely to the left side. Your left hand will still be closed and thumb pointing away from the target. Your left wrist is still flat. Be sure your left arm is folded to the position shown in the picture.

Figure 5-3A DRILL #3 ADD RIGHT HAND. This is exactly the same as DRILL #2 except you grip your extended left thumb with the index, middle, and ring fingers of your right hand, keeping the little finger of the right hand off. At address your right elbow will relax and point toward your right hip.

Figure 5-3B Swing to the top, left wrist flat, right side relaxed just going along for the ride.

Figure 5-3C. Shift from the right to left side returning the back of your left hand square to the target.

Figure 5-3D Same finish as in DRILL #2 except now the right hand is accompanying the left. The right elbow will be relaxed again and pointing downward, not to the side.

Figure 5-4A DRILL #4 CLUB UPSIDE DOWN. With your left hand grip a wood club in the neck so the club is upside down. Add your right hand grip lightly in the fingers, then repeat the positions of the previous drills.

Figure 5-4B Swing to the top with the left wrist flat and the left thumb pointing parallel to the target line.

Figure 5-4C Transfer the weight to the left side, throw your right hand off the club just prior to the impact position, make the back of your left hand face the target at impact.

Figure 5-4D Let your left side continue to its good finish. This should make a whooshing sound if you have generated sufficient speed.

Figure 5-5
DRILL #5 LEAVE THE RIGHT HAND. Do exactly as you did in DRILL #4 except to leave the right hand on the club throughout the swing. Don't exert greater right hand grip pressure that slows the speed and decreases the loudness of the whoosh.

Getting to the Top of the Backswing

You now actually have most of the important elements that are fundamental to a good golf shot: grip, stance, alignment, and footwork. All that remains is to get the club to the top of your swing in the correct plane in a square position and then deliver it to the ball that way.

A very important part of getting the club to the top correctly is found in the takeaway. For the first couple of feet in your backswing, you should try to maintain the same relationship between your left arm and the clubface that you had at address. (Figure 5-9) This means keeping the face in a square position, one that would still be at a right angle to the target if you were to reverse your direction and return the clubface to the ball. To complete this maneuver, take the club back by pushing it away with your left arm supported and aided by your right hand. When the club passes your right leg, the arc of the backswing will start more noticeably upward. The wrists will begin to cock as they near the height of the hip. The correct wrist cock is very simple, but at first may seem a little awkward or unnatural. To practice it, hold your left arm extended in front of you at eye level, with the fist closed but with the thumb extended and pointing upward. Now cock your wrist so that the thumb inclines straight back toward your nose. It won't come very far; in fact, it won't feel like you

Figure 5-6A DRILL #6 RIGHT HAND COMING OFF, #7 IRON. Choke down on your grip for greater control of the now heavier weight in your hand. Swing to the top position you have been practicing. Let your right hand assist in stabilizing the takeaway, completing the backswing and positioning your left wrist correctly. Otherwise let it ride along with the left arm swing.

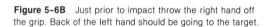

Figure 5-6B Just prior to impact throw the right hand off the grip. Back of the left hand should be going to the target.

Figure 5-6C Finish as in previous drills. Make certain that the last three fingers have not opened up and that your left wrist has not collapsed.

Figure 5-7A DRILL #7 FULL SWING, #7 IRON. From a normal grip position swing the club to the top with the position of your arms, hands, and body just as they have been through the previous six drills.

Figure 5-7B Return through impact with weight to the left and the back of the left hand facing the target.

Figure 5-7C Finish in a comfortable "facing the target" position, as you did during the other drills. *NOW,* put a ball on a tee in the way of the swing you have just practiced.

Figure 5-8
THE FORWARD SWING. (A) The top of the swing. The right leg is slightly flexed but braced. The left knee points to a spot just behind the ball when the shoulders have made their full turn. The left heel is slightly off the ground. (B) The slide turn and pull. The left side begins its lateral slide and turn accompanied by a weight shift and forward pull of the left arm. (C) A wide radius. The left arm continues to pull in an extended position as the weight is being transferred to the left leg. (D) Impact. Contact is made with the ball as the right arm extends and the lower body bows slightly to the left. The head stays ''back.'' (E) Extension and release. The hips turn through as the swing extends toward the target. The left knee is still slightly flexed and the forearms and hands continue their release by rotating over. (F) A strong finish. Good body motion and footwork will result in the right foot finishing on its toe and the right knee and stomach pointing toward the target. A strong extension will bring the hands to a full finish.

have cocked it much at all. Possibly that explains the unnatural feeling. What you will see when you do this correctly is some wrinkles forming under your thumb. If wrinkles appear under your wrist, then you have dorsally flexed your wrist (to the left), a position that encourages one of

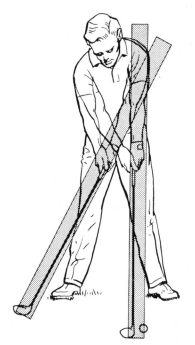

Figure 5-9
Keeping the clubface square in the takeaway.

golf's major errors, the slice. An example of the slice is pictured in Figure 5-10A. To guard against that happening, keep your forearm and wrist in a straight line. You may develop that feeling by practicing the placement of a book flat on the back of your hand so that it covers the wrist and extends from the knuckles to mid-forearm. Cock your thumb back as far as you can, keeping the book firm and flat. This is the position your left hand should be in at the top of the swing. (Figure 5-10B)

The remainder of your backswing will simply be a continuation of the extended left side–dominated motion that is already underway. The takeaway and backswing constitute an armswing that powers the turn of the shoulders, the trunk, and the hips in a chain fashion. Although dominated by the left side, the right hand is quite important during the backswing, not only for what it does but also for what it *shouldn't* do. The role of the right side at this point is mostly to remain passive. The grip in your right hand does stabilize the left in the initial portion of the backswing, helps in getting the backswing completed, and supports the left arm at the top of the backswing. A moderately relaxed right grip allows your right wrist to cock so that your hand is resting correctly under the shaft at the top of the swing. With an absence of tension in your right arm at the top of the swing, the right elbow will point almost toward the ground, a position that has been likened to a waiter carrying a tray. If tension is present

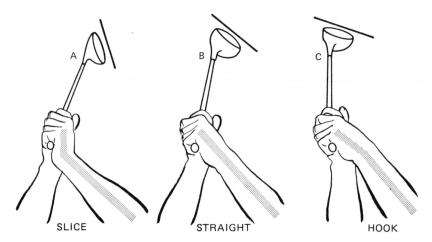

Figure 5-10
Clubface and wrist position at the top of the swing. (A) Open. (B) Square. (C) Closed.

in your right side because you are using your right hand and arm to pick up the club in the backswing, then your right elbow will fly into the air and point directly behind and away from you. Finally don't use the right hand to fan the face open by rolling it to the inside toward your right leg on the takeaway.

Swinging in Plane

One of the principles of swinging that was noted at the beginning of this chapter is to swing the club close to a single plane. Although the plane does change slightly on the downswing from the one taken on the backswing, at this point consider it as being the same as the backswing. A baseball swing at chest height resembles a horizontal plane; an underhand softball pitch is vertical; and the golf swing falls somewhere between the two. Errors result when the swing gets out of plane or "off the track." To find the correct plane, simply imagine the type of spoked wheel (illustrated in Figure 5-11) that is tilted around your body and that points in the direction of your line of flight.

Return and Impact

If you are in the correct position at the top, the rest is much easier. To make a downswing, all you have to do is transfer your weight to the left while pulling with an extended left arm, and let the clubhead swing through the ball to a full finish—more a feeling than a mechanic.

To acquire that feeling, you should understand that the move-

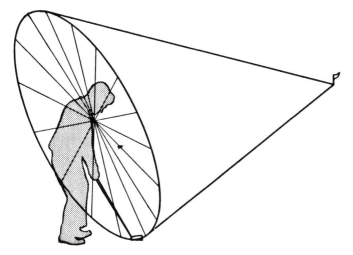

Figure 5-11
The swing plane visualized as extended to the target.

ment from the top of the swing on is primarily one of weight shift, un-coiling, and pulling rather than a pushing or early casting action. The cor-rect sequence of the action—feet, legs, hips, trunk, arms, and hands—blends the forces and brings them to a summation at impact, the moment of truth. In Figure 5-12 I am practicing this critical position by using an Impact Bag.* Note the left and right hand positions in Figure 5-13.

A most helpful drill, practicing the drill 5-6 will make you acutely aware of the uncoiling feeling that comes through the left side. Take your proper grip and stance position. Swing your arms and club away so that your shoulders and hips turn to make a full backswing, your left wrist is cocked in a square position, and your left arm is extended. Start your down-swing with a shift of weight accompanied by the arms starting downward, a lateral slide, and turn of the hips toward the target. Pull, feeling the muscles in your back and particularly those under your left shoulder, until you approach your right hip or thigh. *Keep your wrists fully cocked to this point.* When it seems as though it is almost too late to ever get the club-head through, then let it fly utilizing centrifugal force. To help you realize that it will catch up to your hands without your help, let go with your right hand (in a practice swing) in the impact zone. There is no way you can stop the club from lashing through! You could retard its speed, how-ever, by squeezing with your right hand if it were on the club—which is what the majority of unskilled players do. This experience should dem-onstrate conclusively to you that you won't *consciously* need to hit with your right hand at all to produce distance. You may, and some players do, but you don't need to. The right hand has a role to play in adding power

*Available from Golf Works, 4820 Jackson Town Road, State Route 13, Newark, Ohio 43055.

Figure 5-12
Here is the best practice device I've ever used. It's called an Impact Bag.* There is only one moment of truth in the golf swing—impact. This aid teaches dramatically the feel and position of correct impact.

Figure 5-13
Note the position of the back of the left hand. This is how all the great players look at impact when they are correct.

to the swing, but is best utilized when no concentrated attempt is made to use it for that purpose. Instead, work diligently on strengthening your left side, for the forces generated by the unwinding of your body and pulling action of your whole left side produce the "swinging hit" that is so characteristic of the Snead-like swing.

A natural "release" of the energy that has built up in the swing will also help the clubface to square itself to the ball so that your direction will be true. If the energy is correctly released, you will be able to feel the weight of the clubhead, like a rock on the end of a rope. Trying to "hit at" the ball rather than swing the club produces the tension in your hands that slows the clubhead down. The correct release will allow the club to complete a full follow-through in a natural manner. A good finish indicates the quality of the action that has gone on before.

There is one exception to the type swing we have described. That is when the player, for physical reasons, can wind his body only a moderate amount. Then he must emphasize more the use of an active right-hand leverage-type hit. Still, the left hand must arrive first to get maximum efficiency.

THIS CHAPTER HAS SHOWN YOU THAT:

Individual differences may affect the "mannerisms" in your swing, but there are certain principles in swinging that can't be overlooked.

The golf swing is a roughly circular motion, made in nearly a single plane around a center located near the upper region of the chest.

When you swing, rather than hit, there is a definite feeling of weight at the end of the club that is the result of centrifugal force.

In the swinging hit, the ball seems to jump off the clubface and travel farther than expected for the effort made.

Footwork is the foundation upon which the swing is built. It should be mastered before one attempts hitting balls.

You should be concerned primarily with developing the feeling of a left-sided swing in order to properly balance the role of the right.

6

THE FULL SWING APPLIED TO IRONS AND WOODS

the same principle with adjustments

This chapter will tell you how to apply:
1. The basic swing to both the irons and the woods.
2. The adjustments for each of the two types of shots.
3. The way to achieve the most consistent distance in your shots.

Now that you have been introduced to the principles of the swing and the fundamental preparations that precede it, it's time to apply that knowledge to some golf shots. The answers to the following questions should become clear to you as you progress through the chapter. What two words do you need to think of when first learning to hit an iron shot? Why do some balls that you hit become airborne, while others roll along the ground? What are some of the factors that influence distance, and how are these best applied to the swing?

THE IRONS

Irons are the most versatile clubs in your set because they offer the widest range of trajectory and distance. All irons, however, are designed for one basic purpose: to get the ball onto the green. To do that, you must first learn to get the ball up into the air. But, in one of golf's paradoxes, to get the ball up, you must learn to feel as though you are *hitting it slightly down* as your swing is traveling forward through to the target. To understand the statement "hit it down," look at parts A and B in Figure 6–1 and notice the angle of rebound the ball takes as a result of the swing arc and loft of the clubface. (There are some additional technical reasons controlling the angle of rebound, but they do not contribute to one's under-

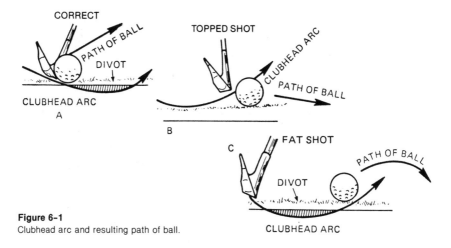

Figure 6-1
Clubhead arc and resulting path of ball.

standing of the swing principle.) In 6–1A the proper arc is shown to reach its lowest point *after* the ball has actually been contacted. This is what we mean by "hitting down." Actually, we always should be trying to swing the club forward, through the ball to the target. But as you develop the correct weight transfer, the center line of your body will be slightly ahead of the ball when it's struck, allowing the club to continue downward before reaching the bottom of its arc. In this way it becomes both a forward swing and a downswing that takes a small grass divot.

You can see the approximate angle of rebound the ball will take because you forced the ball in your downward arc to work itself upward and onto the face. Once the ball is on the clubface, it has no choice but to go up. In essence, then, your job is not to attempt to lift the ball, but to deliver the face down to and through the ball. It is advisable in your practice swing to check to see that your club is taking a divot, ruffling the grass, or (if on a mat) brushing the mat slightly in *front* or to the left of where the ball is resting.

Figure 6–1B and C show the arc that the clubhead takes when you try to *lift* the ball into the air. The result is that the bottom of the arc of the swing is reached *before* the club actually gets to the ball. In Figure 6–1B the leading edge of the club, rather than the clubface, strikes the ball. It makes contact above the ball's center and sends it rebounding in a downward direction. This causes "topping the ball," the most common error of the beginning player. Another shot that is in error for almost the same reason is shown in C. Here the bottom of the arc again is reached before striking the ball, but this time earlier in the swing (usually owing to inadequate weight transfer). The result is the displacement of a great deal of turf behind the ball (called "sclaffing" or "hitting the shot fat") and an accompanying loss of force that sends the ball a shorter distance than it should travel—sometimes only a few feet.

Adjustments Among the Clubs

Now that you are aware of one of the fundamental concepts of hitting successful iron shots—swinging the club so that it results in a slightly downward and toward blow—let's look into the minor changes that are made when you switch from one iron to another. The principles of the swing remain the same for all full golf shots, but you must make some small but important adjustments.

The first adjustment is in the width of your stance. Longer shots require a bigger swing and therefore a wider base from which to secure your balance. The positioning of your feet can also have an effect on the degree to which you can pivot your body. Too wide a stance, however, will restrict the hip turn both on the backswing and follow-through. To see how this works, place your feet in an exaggerated closed position (the left foot ahead of your line of flight), and then see how far you can turn your hips to the right. Now, reverse the line of your feet to an open stance (the left foot withdrawn from your line of flight), and try the same hip turn. It's obvious that your hip turn is much more restricted when you are in the open stance. A restricted hip turn will also restrict the length of the backswing. On short-iron shots, this is good.

The shorter-iron clubs are often used with what is called a "three-quarters swing," which simply means that the club is swung approximately three-quarters as far back as a full swing with a wood. A full 9 iron shot would be a good example of a three-quarters swing. It is also a shot that may employ a slightly open stance to help restrict the pivot. Some top-level players play this shot from an open stance, others from square; but all use a shorter, more controlled swing than with a driver. Conversely, you need the greatest turn and therefore the longest swing and widest stance of the iron clubs with a 2 iron. For all practical purposes, then, we can generalize that your swing is longer and your stance is wider and more square on the long irons than on the short irons.

Another factor that the placement of your feet affects is the degree to which you can strike a downward blow to the ball. In a 9 iron, for example, the center line of the body ends up more to the left at impact because the stance is not wide and your weight can be easily moved to the left. Couple this weight transfer with a more upright swing as a result of having a shorter club, and you end up hitting the ball a sharply descending blow. The 2 iron swing is less oblique because the club is longer and also because the wider stance does not permit a heavy concentration of weight on the left foot either at address or during the swing. A 2 iron shot will therefore take less of a divot than a more lofted club.

Three Key Words for Iron Play

When you practice hitting balls, start with a 7 iron because it is about the easiest club to hit. A 5 iron would come second on my own list of choices if a 7 were not available. If you are like every other golfer, at the beginning you will produce your share of shots that don't get into the air but rather go skimming or bounding along the ground because they have been "topped." You'll go a long way toward eliminating this mistake by concentrating on three key words, which can be applied to all iron shots. The three key words are *left, downward,* and *through.*

When you say "left," you should picture a shift of weight to the left foot and an unwinding of the trunk using the back muscles, plus a pulling of the club with the left arm. "Downward" should simply keep you alert to the fact that you must deliver the face of the club down to the ball with your arms at extension. In this kind of swing, you should feel almost as if you are trying to squeeze or pinch the ball between the clubface and the grass. And "through" should be a part of every swing. Not "to" but "through." The result will be an on-balance full finish. It is important when considering these three key words that you think first "left" and then "downward" and "through" together. Reversing this order and thinking "downward" first would cause you to sclaff, or hit behind the ball.

THE WOODS

For many people the most satisfying feeling in golf is to catch a drive fully in the clubface and send it soaring far down the center of the fairway. Even the earliest of written accounts of the game show that golfers were fascinated with distance. There was much made of prodigious driving feats, and a long hitter was envied.

Though wood clubs are the long artillery in your set, they are also a source of frustration for many golfers. I have had people come to me for a lesson and say, "I can hit the irons without trouble, but I just can't hit the woods. Should you swing differently with the woods than you do with the irons?" The answer, basically, is "no." You employ the same principle for swinging in all of your full shots. Of course, you must make a few adjustments because of the length of the club and, in some cases, because the ball is teed up; but otherwise the mechanics are the same.

The Tee Shot

One solid fundamental to which you have just been introduced in the full swing is that you hit slightly down and through on all of your iron shots. This feeling may apply also to the fairway woods, depending upon how the ball lies, but *not* to the tee shot.

Overcoming distance is an important part of your goal in driving a golf ball from a tee. Certainly you must keep the ball out of trouble, but a nice straight drive 150 yards down the fairway on a 400-yard hole is not nearly as advantageous as is a 250-yard one on the edge of the rough. To get the most distance from your drives, tee the ball so that at least one-half of it is showing above the clubface at address. (Figure 6–2) You will want to position the ball far enough forward in your stance that the ball is struck at the bottom of the arc of your swing. Hitting the ball at the lowest point of the arc, a level blow, decreases its backspin, which is a factor in controlling roll on the fairways. Just where you place the ball will depend upon how strongly you shift your weight to the left and where you get the best results. Generally, this is in line with your left heel or slightly back from it.

In addition to positioning the ball differently on the drive, you should make two other small adjustments in preparing for the tee shot. First, stand farther from the ball because the club is longer. (Use the same technique for body positioning that was described in Chapter 4.) Second, widen your stance so that the insides of your feet are about shoulder width apart. Since the tee shot employs the longest swing, it requires the most balance and therefore the widest stance. But a note of caution: Reaching for the ball past your natural arm hang and standing with your feet wider than shoulder width are common mistakes for the new player.

Fairway Woods

The wood shot from the grass, called a "fairway wood," is one of the most feared golf strokes for the novice player. There is no club in the bag with which he tops the ball more often. Many players put their fairway woods (3, 4, and 5) back in the bag and choose instead a 3 or 4 iron. This may be temporarily effective, but it is not smart for the long term. You should learn how to hit the fairway wood shots, because you will eventually find

Figure 6-2
Proper height to tee the ball.

them easier to play than the long irons. A fairway wood, like a long iron, is hit only slightly down and through, more like it is being swept from the grass. The adjustments that you make are to stand farther from the ball than with a shorter iron and to play the ball a bit farther back in your stance than you do on your driver—about two to four inches inside the left heel.

There is reason to believe that problems other than the added mechanical difficulty due to the length of the club might also make the fairway wood shot difficult at first. Psychologically, the player looks at the club, recognizes it as a wood, and instinctively swings it in the characteristic way he swings for his teed drives: Trying to sweep the ball up, he swings a little too high; trying for distance, he swings a little too hard. Because the ball is not teed, the fairway shot does not allow the player as much margin of error. Add to that the fear of mishitting the ball, which has been reinforced by past performance, and the player will usually tighten up just before making contact with the ball, thus shortening his muscles and pulling his club upward, away from and above the center of the ball. The result is a topped shot. To develop the confidence that is needed to hit the fairway wood shot well, choke the club to about the length of a 7 iron and imagine you are swinging the 7 iron for a few shots. Practice this until you have the confidence that the ball will get up into the air with the wood club if you just deliver the clubface a bit more *down* to it before following through.

Distance: The Wood Shot's Great Temptation

Distance is a prime objective of the drive, but how are you to achieve it? A friend of mine once described golf as "a game in which you try to hit a ball just a little harder than you are humanly capable of doing." That's what makes the woods difficult for many people. They try to hit rather than swing, and they try to hit too hard! The harder you try to hit the ball, the less chance you have of contacting it squarely. Frequent mishits produce an overall average distance that is actually shorter than one with a more controlled, repeating, steady swing. Since the club's extra length makes it more difficult to contact the ball squarely, try to make a full-motion "slinging" feel rather than a muscularly tight attempt to "hit hard." The term "slinging" implies winding, unwinding, and throwing or releasing something. This concept may help you reduce arm and hand tension, which will produce a purer swinging motion.

Distance is a result of two primary factors (if we disregard, for the moment, the weight of the clubhead): (1) the velocity of the clubhead and (2) the squareness of contact. You may have heard someone exclaim after a particularly long drive that he didn't even try to swing hard. This can be explained quite simply. With a more free-flowing, yet in-control, swinging motion, you have a much better chance of making square contact with

Figure 6–3
A true swinging motion will bring you to a balanced, comfortable finish position. Fix this picture indelibly in your mind and attempt to create this feeling in your own swing.

the ball and getting your best clubhead speed. Tension-filled efforts to hit home runs off the tee produce golf's most frequent "mistake shots," like hitting the ball on the toe or the heel, topping or skying it, or prematurely releasing the power from your wrists so that you either hit behind it or get "powder-puff" drives. Distance is best developed by a well-timed, gradually accelerating, swinging-slinging feeling. (Figure 6–3)

WHEN YOU GET OUT ON THE COURSE REMEMBER THAT:

A ball that goes in the air when you strike it is a result of the loft in the clubface rather than any attempt by you to lift it.

An open stance tends to restrict the length of the backswing, which is one reason it is frequently used in short-iron play.

The three key words to consider once you start hitting iron shots from the grass are *left, downward,* and *through.*

You should position your fairway wood more like your long iron than like your driver.

Full, uninhibited swings that you can repeat produce more consistent overall distance than attempts to "hit the ball."

7

THE SHORT GAME

where score can be influenced most quickly

In learning the basic short shots—the putt, the chip,
and the pitch—you need to:
1. Develop some feeling for when each shot should be used.
2. Identify any gross change in execution
from the full swing.
3. Be aware of the subtle changes in stance
and address for each shot.

One of golf's more appealing characteristics is that it has managed to blend the demand for both power and finesse almost equally into a single game. No knowledgeable golfer denies the advantage of being able to strike the ball a great distance. Neither does he ignore the numerical importance of the shorter shots in the game, which are executed on and around the green.

PUTTING

Someone once suggested that there are two separate games played on a golf course: golf and putting. Golf is played in the air; putting is played along the ground. Their only common feature is the ball.

There are several principles related to the laws of physics that govern the swing, which can be accomplished only when the player performs specific patterns of action. But in putting, as we'll see in a moment, there are really only two imperatives. The style that you adopt to apply these essentials can take a wide variety of forms. By observing some of the great professional players on television, your conclusion may well be, "There is certainly more than one way to roll the ball into the hole." Before revealing the two essential fundamentals, however, let's see how important putting is in determining your score.

The putter is one of the most important clubs in golf! Don't let anyone convince you otherwise. You are allowed to carry a maximum of fourteen clubs in your golf bag. If you consider the approximate number of strokes it would take with each club to shoot 18 holes in 100, your pattern would look something like this: woods (both driver and fairway), 24 strokes; all irons, 38 strokes; putter, 38 strokes. Thirteen of your clubs would absorb 62 shots, and more than one-third of the strokes would be taken with the remaining club: the putter! The better player you become, the greater percentage of your score will be consumed in putting. The fastest reduction in score can invariably be accomplished by improvement on and around the green. That's the real scoring zone.

Two Imperatives

When I was in my teens, I once tried practicing a new putting technique on the rug, using as a target one of the little glasses you can buy at the supermarket that contain cheese. They have an opening slightly larger than the circumference of a golf ball. I was putting from a distance of eight to ten feet and averaging two or three "bull's-eyes" out of five. My mother, not being a golfer, questioned the point of my diversion. I explained that I was practicing my putting and asked her if she wished to try. She accepted and promptly grasped the putter in a most unorthodox way, stood in an awkward-looking position, and produced a terrible stroke that sent the ball right into the glass. Mumbling something about "beginner's luck," I retrieved the ball and placed it five feet farther from the glass for another try. She repeated her technique with exactly the same result. "That doesn't seem so hard," she commented. I was just a bit stunned, for I had been working on some very complicated adjustments in my technique. But my mother, who doesn't even play golf, gripped the club "wrong," stood "wrong," and stroked the ball "wrong," but rolled it dead into the glass twice in succession. She must have done *something* right! Then it occurred to me: (1) she delivered the putter face squarely to the target, and (2) she hit the ball hard enough to get to the glass but not so hard as to go through it. That's really all you have to do in making a putting stroke! And that is precisely what many fine players attempt to do when putting.

Deane Beman, former U.S. Amateur champion, PGA tour player and commissioner, and one of the game's greatest putters, has said that all he really attempts in his stroke is to keep the blade going toward his target and to develop some feel for the distance. It's that simple; but it's not that easy.

You must develop some kind of technique that will allow you to accomplish those two necessities in putting. The following method is *both* simple to understand and easy to learn. You may find another technique more to your liking, but try the following first. The answer to the decision on which method is right for you lies in the bottom of the cup.

The Technique

Standing with your feet about eight inches apart in a square stance, sole your putter in front of your left toe and rest it vertically against your left leg. Now let your arms hang in front of you and gradually bend forward at the waist, flexing the knees until your fingertips can touch the tops of your kneecaps. At this point move your right palm directly onto the grip. Your hand should assume any position that is comfortable in the palm and fingers, as long as it is directed toward the target. Now take the last three fingers and the thumb of your left hand and place them on the grip, sliding your thumb under the hollow made by the crease in the palm of your right hand. This leaves your left index finger still free. Simply lap it over the fingers of the right hand, pointing it in the general direction of the ground in the position that is most comfortable. This is knows as the "reverse overlapping grip." (Figure 7–1) In this position your right elbow will rest almost against the front of your right hip, and your left elbow will assume whatever spot that is natural and comfortable.

Place more weight on the left foot than right to focus your balance and to discourage the strong tendency to sway. The club should be soled as though the ball were being played either inside your left instep or di-

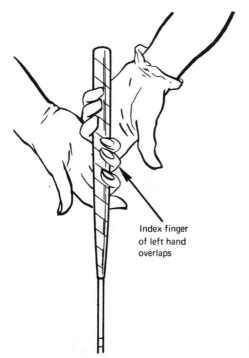

Index finger
of left hand
overlaps

Figure 7–1
Reverse overlapping grip for putting.

rectly in front of your toe, depending upon how much of your weight is on the left foot. You will notice that your left eye is looking almost directly down on the ball. Adjust yourself to a reasonably comfortable position. Now you are ready to putt.

Keeping the Blade Square

One little trick I have learned, which may help you keep the putter blade square, is to place the ball about two feet from the hole. (This is to be done on a level surface.) Rest the blade of the club against the ball and square to the center of the hole. Then, keeping the blade squared, and without a backstroke, briskly push the blade toward the hole. The ball will leave the clubface, which should follow through from six to eight inches. If the terrain is flat and you have kept the blade square, the ball *must* go directly toward the hole. It has no other choice. Repeat this routine several times until you get some feeling for how hard to push. Then, still standing two feet from the hole, swing the blade back away from the ball three to four inches and with a smooth rhythm deliver the putter face squarely to the ball. This movement is made without action from the wrists. The wrists are in a fixed position so that the club, hands, wrists, and arms move in one unit. (Figure 7–2) To continue the feeling of keeping the blade square, gradually move the ball on the same line farther from the hole. As you do so, increase the length of your backstroke slightly with each increase in distance. Concentrate solely on keeping the putter blade moving toward

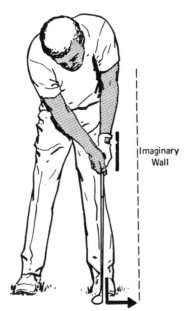

Imaginary
Wall

Figure 7-2
The putting stroke—keeping the blade square.

your target. On very long putts, it may be necessary to hinge the wrists slightly for additional power. As this complicates the task of delivering the clubface squarely, it should be done only when necessary. Don't assume that "wrist putting" is not an acceptable method, for it is. In fact, it is used by some of golf's finest putters. It is simply more difficult for a beginning player, who should be learning to present the face to the target line squarely.

Some people unknowingly close or open the face of the putter on contact with the ball, sending it off the desired line. If you have this problem, practice the following exercise while standing about six inches from a wall. (Figure 7–2) Take your stroke, keeping it low and square, and follow through so that the blade comes to rest flat against the wall. This drill repeated over and over will give you the feeling that you always have the blade moving toward the target.

Learning how hard to hit the ball is more difficult than learning to keep the blade squared. No one can teach you the secret because, first of all, it requires a certain innate touch or judgment of distance that some people find easy and others don't. Second, it requires a great deal of practice to judge distance on long putts over varying terrain and with fluctuating turf conditions. How do you know how hard to hit a putt? As a veteran professional once said, "Practice a few thousand times, and you'll 'know.'" Although this answer is fundamentally true, it is a bit unreasonable for the less experienced. Here are a few hints to help you for the time being.

It should be obvious that on short putts you take a shorter backstroke than on longer ones. But the correct length must come from a sense of feel. One method that I employ on long putts is to break the putt into thirds. If I have a putt of thirty feet, I first take a practice stroke, trying to feel what effort I will have to give the putt to hit it ten feet along the same line; then I repeat this action for twenty feet and finally the full distance. That is the final feeling that I try to develop just before getting over the ball and striking it. These practice strokes should be made with a definite smooth rhythm. Whatever system you develop, it's a good idea to rehearse the feel before you hit the ball. When it feels right, then putt.

Reading the Greens

Not all golf greens are flat, even though they sometimes appear to be that way on television because of the elevated cameras. As a matter of fact, it is more difficult to find a level green than it is to find an uneven one. Undulating greens, however, do not change the two necessary fundamentals for putting: a square face and correct distance judgment. A sloped surface simply alters your aim. You still keep the blade square to the target, but the target is an imaginary one now, rather than an actual one. To allow for curve caused by the green's slope and gravity, you must *estimate* the line that the putt should take. Establishing this guessed line is called "taking borrow for the putt" or "reading the break." On long putts you allow more borrow than on short ones over the same line, because gravity has a greater amount of time to work on the ball. You'll also find at first that you may tend to stroke the ball too easily when traveling uphill and too hard when going down a steep grade. Practice these situations until you have a fairly good idea of how much break and effort to allow. Practicing your putting can be an enjoyable pastime either at the course or at home. Taking pride in your putting will certainly help reduce your scores—but taking those "few thousand" practice putts will help more.

CHIP SHOTS AND PITCH SHOTS

When you find your ball too near the green to take a full swing with any club, yet not in a position where you can putt, you must employ one of the short shots in golf, either a chip or a pitch. Their execution is different from that of the full swing because the stroke is abbreviated, sometimes no longer than that of a putt. The chip and pitch also employ slightly different techniques in "setting up" to hit the shot.

The chip shot is really just an elongated putt with a bit of loft at the beginning. You chip rather than putt when the grass on your line to the hole is too thick and will markedly slow the shot or throw it off target. Employ a club with just enough loft to get the ball comfortably over the longer grass so it can run uninterrupted to the hole. I recommend to my students that they limit their choices to a 6, 8, or pitching wedge for such shots. Far too many novices overuse the high-lofted club in situations where the running shot (which is easier to perform) is all that is necessary.

A great deal of the success of the chip shot depends upon how you set yourself up. The shot is an iron shot, so you should hit it slightly on the downswing. Since power and long distance are not requirements of the chip shot, there is no need for a full swing or any significant transfer of weight. In fact, the less complicated you make the shot, the better. With the ball placed between your feet (which are in an open stance position), put 75 to 85 percent of your weight on your left foot and leave it there. Just as in the full swing, you will find that with the weight to the left, the ball will be struck a slightly downward blow, getting it onto the clubface and up in the air.

Grip down on the club and let your arms hang so they are almost brushing against your thighs. At address, keep your hands well ahead (to the left) of the ball and clubhead. (Figure 7–3A) The stroke on chip shots is very similar to that made in the putt. No wrist action is necessary unless the distance becomes a major factor. The only fundamental difference from the putt in this stroke is that on the chip the ball is a slight descending blow. This is facilitated by placing your weight to the left, having the

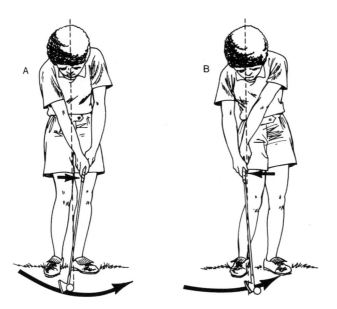

Figure 7-3
Stance and address for the chip and pitch shots. (A) Correct address: Player
encourages stroke down and through. (B) Incorrect address: Player is scooping.

ball played farther back in your stance near the center, and having your
hands stay ahead of the clubhead throughout the shot. Allowing your wrists
to break on the forward swing in an effort to *scoop* the ball upward is the
most common error in the chip shot. (Figure 7-3B)

When the shot becomes longer and the ball has to be lofted more
into the air, it is usually referred to as a "pitch shot." The technique of
setting up is almost exactly the same as for the chip: open stance, weight
left, and hands ahead of the clubhead. In this shot as well, the ball is struck
a downward blow. Since the pitch shot usually requires more of a swinging
effort to achieve the required distance, you must use a little bit of your
footwork action and a cocking of the wrists in its execution. Even if some
weight transfer is needed, keep as much of the weight as possible to the
left throughout the swing. The best rule to remember regarding both the
chip and the pitch shots is to keep them simple by using only as much
wrist action and weight transfer as is necessary for the distance.

Knowing which club to use in which situation is sometimes puz-
zling for the beginning player. A general rule of thumb is to use as little
loft as possible and to allow the ball to roll when you can. (Figure 7-4)
Some pros, however, have developed such confidence in a certain club
from continual practice (such as the pitching wedge or sand wedge) that
they use it for almost every shot around the greens. Perhaps if they had
spent an equal amount of time practicing with the lower-lofted clubs, they
might now be better short-game players. However, this is a moot point.

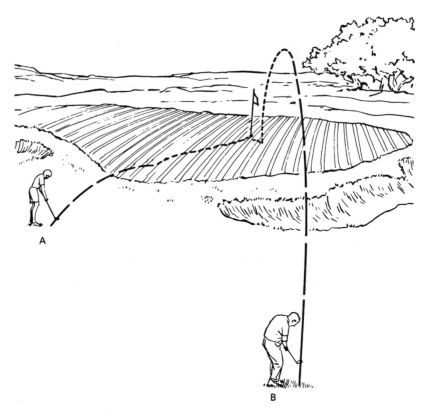

Figure 7-4
Club selection around the green. (A) Chip or chip-and-run shot: 6, 8, or pitching wedge. (B) Pitch shot: pitching wedge or sand wedge.

For you, it is wiser to learn to pitch and chip with the clubs I've suggested, plus the sand wedge for pitching, and then fit the selection of the club to the situation.

The Sand Shot

Most golfers have at best only a foggy notion of how to consistently execute a bunker or sand trap shot successfully. Hitting from the sand is really not as difficult as the weekend player makes it seem. But you must know the mechanics and then spend a little time practicing them. Without the knowledge or the practice, a sand trap experience can be very frustrating and stroke consuming. It certainly doesn't have to be.

A sand wedge makes sand play much easier. This is a club with a heavy, specially contoured sole that deflects itself off the sand rather than digging too deeply into it. A pitching wedge or 9 iron could be used in a sand trap if you opened the face, but it would certainly be more difficult to use than the sand wedge.

The techniques for executing the shot are simply:

1. Establish a firm footing by working your feet into the sand.
2. Take an open stance and position the ball near your left instep, farther forward than for a pitch shot.
3. Place your weight slightly to the left side as in a pitch shot.
4. Pick a spot from three to four inches behind the ball in the sand as the target that you are going to hit.
5. Open your clubface so the leading edge will not dig but rather allow the club to bounce.
6. Take a swing that picks the clubhead up more abruptly in the back-swing and delivers a bit more downward blow than in the pitch shot.
7. Finish the swing.

This technique is used when the ball is lying flat on top of the sand. The shot will stop quickly when it hits the green. If the ball is buried, square the face and move your hands ahead to lower the leading edge so it will dig. The deeper it is buried, the more dig you will need. Expect the ball to roll after it comes out. In most cases, *swing through the sand. Do not chop your club into the sand and stop when you meet resistance.* The only exception is when the ball is deeply buried and you must dig deeply with great force. A few practice sessions in the sand will tell you how hard you need to swing.

The first step to success in hitting the greenside bunker shot is to understand that you *don't* hit the ball—you hit the sand, which acts as a

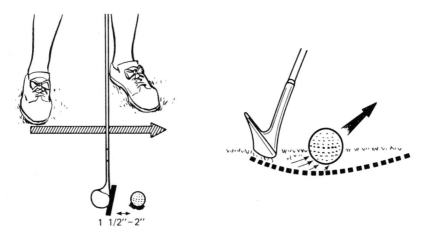

Figure 7-5
Sand trap shot—hitting a target.

buffer between the ball and the clubface. The trick to hitting the shot is to imagine you are just trying to swing the club to a good finish over jyour left shoulder and to throw some sand on the green by swinging through a spot three to four inches behind the ball. (Figure 7–5) Focus your attention on "spanking" your club a little down and through this target during the swing. It will make the trap shot much simpler.

You Should Now Realize That:

One of the most important clubs in your bag from a scoring standpoint is the putter. It should consume a proportionate amount of your practice time.

There are many things you *could* think of when putting, but there are only two you *must* do after reaching the green: Keep the putter blade square to the target, and judge and hit the ball with the right amount of effort.

A chip shot is executed much like a putt except that you set up differently to the ball. The pitch shot is an elongated chip using a more lofted club, with cocked wrists.

The club you select around the green depends on both the situation and your ability to handle the club.

The trick to hitting a sand shot lies in being able to set up correctly, then hitting a spot in the sand behind the ball and swinging your club through it to a good finish.

8

RULES AND ETIQUETTE

golf's laws and manners

This chapter will introduce you to:
1. *The historical development of the rules.*
2. *The principles upon which these rules are based.*
3. *A practical application of both rules and etiquette.*
4. *The most commonly confronted rules situations.*
5. *Safety practices both on the course*
   and during instruction.

"It has been estimated that the golfer's chances of making a hole-in-one are much greater than the probability that he will read the rule book" (Graffis 1965, p. 168). This is unfortunate, for cor.tained in the USGA's annual paperback called *Rules of Golf* (available at all golf shops) are the wisdom and experience of generations of players who have attempted to make the game equitable for all, at every course in the world, under all possible conditions. You would think that the official rule book must compare in size with the unabridged *Webster's Collegiate Dictionary*. The fact is that it is small enough to fit comfortably in your back pocket or golf bag, right where it should be when you play.

DEVELOPMENT OF THE RULES

The first code of rules was born out of necessity in 1774. The gentlemen golfers of Edinburgh wished to have an interclub match with other players from surrounding golf establishments. Since each club had developed its own peculiar set of customs and traditions that were familiar only to its "own," some common ground of understanding was necessary to ensure an orderly match. Thus, a code of thirteen rules was established and sent to the contestants. After 200 + years of golfing, nine of those original rules are still in effect.

This early gathering of rule makers probably never considered the possibility that these rules for their local competition would be applicable to golf all over the world. Contributed to and revised by the Royal and Ancient Club (R&A) at St. Andrews, the Edinburgh rules set the tone for the first universally applied code in 1882. By 1902 the thousands of players who were active in the game had discovered numerous situations that were not specifically covered in the rule book. These cases were placed before a rules committee for a decision.

Similar committees from the USGA and R&A have been rendering decisions ever since.

NATURE OF THE RULES

There are five principles upon which rules are based:

1. You must play the ball as it lies.
2. You must play the course as you find it.
3. You cannot advance the ball without striking it.
4. There is a basic difference between match play and stroke play. Match play is man to man, hole by hole; no one else is affected. Stroke play is on total score, each player against the field. Consequently, rules differ somewhat for the two forms.
5. A hazard is special ground.

The basic purpose of the rules is simply to make sure that everyone plays the same game. Don't assume that golf rules always legislate against you. Just like laws, they exist not only to censure you, but also to protect and guarantee *your* rights. Let's take an example of a common rule that is frequently violated and little understood:

Rule 13–4: Before making a stroke at a ball which lies in or touches a hazard . . . the player shall not: a. Test the condition of the hazard or any similar hazard. b. Touch the ground in the hazard or water in the water hazard with a club or otherwise, or c. Touch or move a *loose impediment* lying in or touching the hazard.

The purpose of a hazard is to penalize an errant, poorly played shot. If your opponent drives a wild shot into a trap so that his ball is buried in the sand, he should pay the penalty of playing it from that spot. However, without the rule barring touching the sand or soling the club, he could press down the sand or even dig around in the hazard without touching or moving the ball but significantly improving his lie. Similarly, in a grassed hazard, the player, before his shot, could use the club as a scythe. In either case the spirit of the law has been violated. That's why

Figure 8-1
In the middle of the picture you can see a ball resting in a footprint. The rules do not allow
relief from this condition or from the loose impediments on the right: a rock, stick, pine cone,
and leaf, but you can move the obstructions such as the rake, pencil, cup, and golf ball
sleeve on the left. If your ball moves in the process, replace it.

hazards are sometimes called "holy" or "untouchable ground." But there
are some exceptions. (Figure 8–1)

GOOD MANNERS ON THE COURSE

Golf's unwritten rules are called "golf etiquette." That is not to say that
the rules of etiquette haven't been written down, but rather that they
aren't really *rules* at all. They are suggestions. No one has ever been dealt
penalty strokes for poor manners on the course. You can't legislate good
behavior—but you can expect it!

Etiquette simply means consideration of the course and of others.
The problem is that when you are playing a new game, you may not be
aware of the particular behavior pattern that constitutes a breach of etiquette. I wouldn't expect a brand-new golfer to know enough to stand so
that his shadow doesn't fall across the line of my putt, or where to stand
when we are teeing off, or when to repair ball marks and divots. But, again,
I'd expect him to find out—soon!

Golf is social, yet individual. You play with others and at the same
time against yourself and the course. For that reason you very seldom mind
golfing with a player of less ability. But you don't enjoy a round with an
ill-mannered player, regardless of his golf prowess.

LEARNING THE RULES

A golf rule book actually contains several items. Among them are:

1. Directions on how to use the book
2. The etiquette of the game
3. Definitions of key terms applying to the rules
4. A thorough cross indexing
5. Changes in the rules from the year before
6. Special notes on such items as amateur status, gambling, lightning protection, and approved equipment
7. The rules themselves

The rule book is small but it is not easy reading—that is, unless you are a lawyer. There are two rules books with illustrations that I recommend: *The New Rules of Golf,* by Tom Watson with Frank Hannigan published by the USGA and *Golf Rules in Pictures* by the National Golf Foundation. If you become a serious tournament competitor, you should definitely learn the complete rules. A new player needs to become acquainted with only the most common rules and etiquette situations. Listed below are (1) definitions of rules terminology, (2) examples of the more frequently violated rules and etiquette procedures, and (3) additional information pertaining to rules and conduct on the course in general. Given a golf rules and etiquette quiz, your knowledge of this brief list would make you a slight favorite to outscore 75 percent of the nation's golfers. Applying this knowledge to your game will make golf more enjoyable for you, your companions, and your fellow golfers.

COMMON RULES: DEFINITIONS

Advice. "Advice" is any counsel or suggestion that could influence a player in determining his play, the choice of a club, or the method of making a *stroke.* Information on the rules or on matters of public information, such as the position of hazards or the flagstick on the putting green, is not advice.

Casual water. "Casual water" is any temporary accumulation of water on the *course* that is visible before or after the player takes his *stance* and is not in a *water hazard.* Snow and ice are either casual water or *loose impediments,* at the option of the player. Dew is not casual water.

Ground under repair. "Ground under repair" is any portion of the *course* so marked by order of the committee or so declared by its authorized representative. It includes material piled for removal and a hole made by a greenskeeper, even if not so marked. Stakes and lines defining ground under repair are in such ground.

Hazards. A "hazard" is any *bunker* or *water hazard.*

Loose impediments. "Loose impediments" are natural objects such as stones, leaves, twigs, branches, and the like; dung; and worms and insects and casts or heaps made by them, provided they are not fixed or growing, are not solidly embedded, and do not adhere to the ball. Sand and loose soil are loose impediments on the *putting green,* but not elsewhere. Snow and ice are either *casual water* or loose impediments, at the option of the player. Dew is not a loose impediment.

Lost ball. A ball is "lost" if: (1) It is not found or identified as his by the player within five minutes after the player's side or his or their caddies have begun to search for it; or (2) the player has put another ball into play under the rules, even though he may not have searched for the original ball; or (3) the player has played any stroke with a *provisional ball* from the place where the original ball is likely to be or from a point nearer the hole than that place, whereupon the provisional ball becomes the *ball in play.* Time spent in playing a *wrong ball* is not counted in the five-minute period allowed for search.

Obstructions. An "obstruction" is anything artificial, including the artificial surfaces and sides of roads and paths, except: (1) objects defining *out-of-bounds,* such as walls, fences, stakes, and railings; (2) any part of an immovable artificial object that is out-of-bounds; and (3) any construction declared by the committee to be an integral part of the course.

Outside agency. An "outside agency" is any agency not part of the match or, in stroke play, not part of a competitor's side, and includes a referee, a marker, an observer, and a forecaddie. Neither wind nor water is an outside agency.

Penalty stroke. A "penalty stroke" is one added to the score of a player or *side* under certain rules. In a threesome or foursome, penalty strokes do not affect the order of play.

Provisional ball. A "provisional ball" is played under Rule 27–2 for a ball that may be *lost* outside a *water hazard* or may be *out-of-bounds.* It ceases to be a provisional ball when the rule provides either that the player continue play with it as the *ball in play* or that it be abandoned.

Rub of the green. A "rub of the green" occurs when a ball in motion is accidentally deflected or stopped by any *outside agency.*

Stroke.   A "stroke" is the forward movement of the club made with the intention of fairly striking at and moving the ball.

Teeing ground.   The "teeing ground" is the starting place for the hole to be played. It is a rectangular area two clublengths in depth, the front and the sides of which are defined by the outside limits of two tee markers. A ball is outside the teeing ground when all of it lies outside the teeing ground.

Through the green.   "Through the green" is all of the golf course with the exception of the teeing ground, the putting green of the hole being played, and any hazard on the course.

RULES FREQUENTLY VIOLATED

You Are Not Allowed to . . .

Take practice shots on the course.   Practice shots are not permitted during the play of a hole. Thus, a second drive from the first tee (commonly called a "mulligan"), while counting only one stroke, is in violation of the rules (Rule 7).

Improve your lie anywhere on the course.   You may not improve your lie by touching the ball or by altering the condition of the course. This includes stepping down on the turf behind the ball in either the fairway or the rough, parting the long grass in the rough to get a better swing at the ball, and nudging your ball with the clubhead onto some better turf. The most frequent and allowable exception to this rule is when, for the protection of the course or because of extremely poor playing conditions, the local course recommends the playing of "preferred" or improved lies, called "winter rules" (Appendix I).

Change balls during the play of a hole.   Unless your ball becomes damaged and unfit for play or is lost, you may not switch balls until the hole is completed. Using a special ball for putting is a rule violation (Rule 5).

Play a ball from outside the course boundaries.   If your ball comes to rest outside the stakes, fences, or walls that mark the boundaries of the course, you must abandon it and play another shot from the previous spot. The penalty for hitting out-of-bounds is loss of distance plus one penalty stroke added to the two shots that were played (Rule 27).

Concede putts to yourself of any length. The playing of a hole concludes when your ball drops into the cup, not before. You may not "give" yourself putts of any length. Only when an opponent in match play concedes a putt are you permitted to not hole out (Rules 3 and 16).

Agree to waive the rules of golf. You may not by mutual agreement with your partner or opponent agree to waive the rules or the penalties associated with the rules in determining your score. Agreeing to not count a complete miss when intending to hit the ball would be an example of such a violation (Rule 1).

Sole your club in a hazard. Since soling your club in a grass or sand hazard could improve the condition of your lie, it is forbidden by the rules and penalized by two strokes in stroke play or the loss of the hole in match play (Rule 13).

Receive from or give advice to your opponent. Asking your opponent or another competitor during the play of a round what club he hit or how he played a given shot violates the rules. You are allowed to receive information only from your partner and your caddie and may give it only to your partner (Rule 8).

According to the Rules You May . . .

Remove loose impediments that interfere with your play. As long as you don't move the ball in so doing, loose impediments may be lifted. The exception to this rule is when both your ball and the impediment lie in a hazard (Rule 23).

Cause the ball to fall from the tee while addressing it, without penalty. Penalties for accidentally moving the ball apply only when the ball is in play. A ball is not in play until a player has made a stroke on the teeing ground. Addressing the ball does not constitute a stroke (Rule 18).

Play a provisional ball when you believe yours to be lost or out-of-bounds. When you are unsure as to whether your ball may have gone out-of-bounds or be lost, play a provisional ball. If you find that the original ball is lost or out-of-bounds, you may then play the provisional ball without having to walk back to the tee (you are lying 3). If you find your first ball and it is in play, you should abandon the provisional ball with no penalty (Rule 27).

Use any club you wish to play a shot. No rule dictates the choice of clubs you must make. An iron or fairway wood may be used from the tee rather than a driver, or a putter may be used in a sand trap rather than a sand wedge.

Declare a ball unplayable and lift it under penalty of one stroke. If your ball comes to rest where you deem it improbable that you could successfully hit it, you may declare it unplayable. Add one penalty stroke and take one of the following three options: (1) Drop the ball two club lengths away from where it rested but no nearer the hole; (2) drop the ball back away from where the ball originally lay, staying in a direct line with the pin, going as far back as you need to get relief; (3) go back to the spot where the shot was originally played and play from that point. The player should choose the option that is to his greatest advantage (Rule 27).

Get relief from an "obstruction" with no penalty. Obstructions are not on the course to add to the natural and artificial hazards of play. You may move an obstruction that interferes with your stroke. In the event it is immovable, find your nearest point of relief (no nearer the hole) and, within one club length of that spot, drop the ball (Rule 24).

Lift and clean the ball on the putting green. A player may lift and clean his ball on the putting green at any time. When lifted, the ball should be marked with a small coin at the backside base of the ball. The coin may be moved one or two putter head lengths over if it interferes with the line of a fellow player's putt (Rule 16).

ETIQUETTE FREQUENTLY VIOLATED

You Should Not . . .

Disturb another player who is in the process of making a stroke. Talking, moving around, and standing in a player's line of vision while he is making a stroke are all considered to be poor manners in golf.

Play a stroke until the players in front of you are clearly out of your reach. If your ball does appear to be in danger of striking someone, holler loudly and immediately the universal warning cry of golf, *"fore!"* If *you* hear someone shout *"fore!"* turn your back to the direction from which the voice came, cover your head, and make yourself as small as possible.

Damage the green with your equipment. Do not set your bag on the green, pull a hand cart across the green, or drag your spiked shoes, kneel, jump, or step on the edges of the holes on a green.

Hold up play on the course. It is good manners as well as a rule to play the game without delay. If you are not keeping up with the normal pace of play on the course and there are players following you, let them go through to fill up the empty holes ahead. If your group loses a ball, wave the following players through while you search for it, letting them finish the hole before you continue.

You Should . . .

Leave the course in as good condition, or better, as you find it. Care of the course should be the concern of all golfers. You can do your part by replacing any divots you take on the tee or through the green, fixing ball marks on the green, and raking any sand traps from which you play. The more conscientious player will also go the "second mile" and repair damage done by other golfers. (Figure 8–2)

Observe the proper order of hitting. When on the tee, recognize the order of hitting by the honor determined from the previous hole's low scores. During the play of the hole, let the player farthest from the flagstick play first. In your eagerness to play your ball, do not get so far ahead of the other players that you appear unconcerned over their results. On the other hand, be ready to hit when it is your turn.

Figure 8-2
It only takes a few seconds to repair your footprints and rake the bunker back into good condition.

Become familiar with the etiquette for the putting green. The putting green has its own etiquette situations. You should be aware that the following are violations of golfing etiquette: standing so that your shadow crosses someone's putting line; leaving your ball in the cup after holing out; not marking your ball when it interferes with another player's stroke; failing to tend the flag for fellow players farther from the hole; and stepping in someone else's putting line.

ADDITIONAL RULES INFORMATION

Carry no more than fourteen clubs.

Strike at the ball with the head of the club. Do not push, scrape, or spoon it.

Don't use artificial devices for measuring distance or weather conditions.

If your ball comes to rest on the wrong putting green, drop off (no penalty).

You may strike the flagstick from off the green without penalty. Striking it from on the green penalizes the player two strokes in medal play and the loss of the hole in match play.

If you strike someone else's ball while playing on the putting green, you are penalized two strokes in medal play or the loss of the hole in match play.

GOLF'S MAJOR PROBLEM: SLOW PLAY

A sign on the first tee of a well-known Scottish golf course reads, "A Round of Golf Takes 3 Hours." That's for eighteen holes, not nine. You'll find that hard to believe and harder yet to accomplish on your first few rounds of the course. But it can be done when you know how to do it. Why, then, you may ask, does it sometimes take five hours to tour the local links?

One of the prime reasons is television. Too many amateur players mimic the professional ritualism that they see on their television sets on weekends. If you were putting for 240,000 dollars as Jack Nicklaus was on the final hole of the 1984 "Skins Game," you too might take a little extra time to survey the shot. But you aren't. Even if your were, it might do you more harm than good anyway. Alex Smith, two-time U.S. Open champion, had a favorite saying about putting: "If you are going to miss 'em, miss 'em quick!"

Putting is one obviously time-consuming place on the course. There are other situations in the game that are also "time wasters." You can overcome them if you apply these suggestions:

1. Know when it is your turn and be ready to hit. You may have to move slightly out in front of someone else who is playing his shot. This is an acceptable practice, provided you are safely to the side and are not disturbing him.

2. When you hit the shot, watch it finish and spot it with some landmark.

3. If walking, walk briskly between shots. The exercise will do you good.

4. When on the green, place your clubs or golf car between the green and the next tee so that you may leave directly. Leave the green immediately when finished. This is not the place to mark your scorecard.

5. Take your practice swings when you won't hold up your group or distract anyone.

It's true that golf courses are being built that are increasingly longer in yardage than they were at the time the three-hour round was the custom. But the number of holes hasn't increased. It's still eighteen, and 500 extra yards of walking shouldn't take two hours. As a parting thought, the world record for playing eighteen holes on foot on a course of over 6,000 yards in length was set in 1931 by Lee Richardson of Cape Town, South Africa. Richardson, a member of the South African Olympic track team, hit all shots with a single club, allowing the ball to stop before striking it again. He completed the round in thirty-one minutes, twenty-two seconds.

A LESSON ON SAFETY

If you think of golf as a fundamentally safe game, you are correct. Considering the number of players and hours spent on a golf course, the accident rate is low. The accidents that do occur, however, can be serious. Your awareness of the following safety hints could save you or some other player from an unnecessary and unfortunate accident.

During Play or Practice

1. Do not hit a ball when there is a chance that you might strike someone playing in front of or adjacent to you.

2. If you strike a ball inadvertently toward another player, shout *"fore,"* loudly and early enough for him to react. It's golf's universal warning cry of "look out" or "beware be*fore.*"

3. If you hear *"fore"* while you are playing, do *not* turn to see who yelled, but rather turn your back to the origin of the cry, cover your head, and make yourself as small as possible.

4. Never approach from the rear a golfer who is addressing the ball or is about to make a practice swing.

5. Before making a practice swing yourself, particularly on the tee ground or the practice range, look around you to see that no one is nearby.

6. Do not swing a club toward anyone who is standing near. Your hands often perspire, making the grip slippery and increasing the possibility that you

might lose the club. In addition, clubheads have been known to crack and come off later in a practice swing.

In Unusual Weather

1. If an electrical storm occurs while you are on the golf course, get inside immediately. Several people are killed by lightning on golf courses each year because they did not take adequate precautionary measures. If you cannot get in, stay away from your clubs, which are natural lightning rods, and don't select a small, exposed shelter or a lone tree for cover. The safest places for shelter outside of a building are in dense woods, at the foot of a hill or depression, or flat on the ground.

2. Be cautious in extreme heat about "overplaying." The challenge of the game may tempt you to play in conditions that can overtax you physically.

During Class Instruction

1. If you are taking instruction as part of a golf school or class, carefully obey those safety rules that are explained to you in your early sessions.

2. Do not leave the range or hitting area to go ahead and retrieve a ball or divot until the whole group has been released to do so.

3. Stop swinging when the instructor requests the group to do so. The temptation to hit "just one more shot" can lead to an injury.

When Riding in a Golf Car

1. If you find it necessary to use a golf car, keep your feet inside. Crushed ankles and broken legs are the most common golf car injuries.

2. Don't speed! Golf cars are easily tipped over, especially if someone is driving too fast and hits a bump.

3. Try to avoid parking on steep inclines or crossing them laterally.

4. Make sure that you know how to stop and start the car and how to operate and set the brakes before you get onto the course.

This Chapter Has Informed You That:

It does not take long to learn the basic rules that govern the great majority of your playing situations.

The basic purpose of the rules is simply to see that everyone plays the same game.

A major problem that faces the game of golf is slow play.

Golfing etiquette consists of a standard of good manners based upon courteous and considerate treatment of others.

Though generally a safe game, golf participation has produced some serious accidents that could have been avoided with the proper precautions.

9

GETTING OUT TO PLAY

testing what you have learned

To help you over the on-course obstacles, this chapter will:
1. Suggest some pointers to prepare you for play.
2. Sketch a mythical three holes played by a new golfer.

The preliminaries are over. In the first eight chapters of this book, you have been introduced to the game of golf and given some essential information that should be of value to you in making golf fun from the start. Now it's time to play.

If you have been on the golf course a few times already, then you know that golf provides a great variety of situations to challenge you and enough satisfying moments to bring you back. Most of the shots demand simply the normal execution of the swing on which you have been working, but some are special and have special results. For example, golfers dream of making a hole-in-one, and over 35,000 will achieve that dream this season. In fact, one player recently accomplished that feat the first time on a golf course on his very first swing. Your concern on your early trips around the course is less likely to be with holes-in-one than with questions such as: Will I hit the ball? Do I know enough about the rules? Will I be faced with shots that I have never practiced? Could I possibly make a par? Will I enjoy it? Will I be nervous? These questions can be answered only when you get out and play the game.

Call the course in advance to see if reservations are required. If they are, make your starting time by phone unless the course takes them only in person. In some cases, primarily at public courses in heavily populated areas, a deposit is necessary. If you are playing with someone but do not have a complete foursome, you may expect to be asked to pair up with two other players or to add a single to your group. This again would be particularly true of a public facility at a peak playing time. If you absolutely do not wish to include strangers (although you'll find it turns out to be a pleasant experience 90 percent of the time), you might check with the course to see when it is least busy. If you are alone and have no one to play with, ask the shop if they will pair you up with someone, telling them at what level you play so they can try to find a golfer close to your playing ability.

You may be unsure as to what equipment you will need and what is available at the course. If you don't own clubs, check to see if the course will rent equipment to you. Borrowing someone else's gear can be embarrassing and expensive if you happen to break or lose a club. Golf shoes, though helpful, are not required. Some courses do have regulations on footwear, however. To be on the safe side, don't wear boots or any kind of spike-heeled shoes, cleated shoes other than golf shoes (e.g., baseball or football shoes), or ripple soles that have sharply defined lines that might imprint the greens.

Balls, tees, and other accessories are in plentiful supply at almost every pro shop. Tell the professional or shop attendant your skill level and ask him to suggest the type of balls for you to buy. You'll need more than one!

After you have checked in at the pro shop and reported to the starter, you will know your turn on the first tee. If you have arrived at the course early enough, hit a few practice shots, provided facilities are available to do so. If there is no range or practice area, spend your time on putting and hitting some short chip shots. When the group before you is on the tee, you can go through your practice swinging warm-up routine, making certain that you are safely away from others. By doing this warm-up early, you'll find that when it is your turn to hit you haven't occupied your entire time with introductions, finding a tee, getting your glove on, and locating a pencil for the scorecard. Now, let's play an imaginary three holes in which some of the situations that you may face on the course are confronted.

FIRST TEE PREPARATIONS

Identify your golf ball by name and number and inform your playing companions so that two of you don't use the exact same type balls. If two balls are identical, change one so they don't become mixed during play. Decide who shall have the "honor" of hitting first. This is usually decided on the first hole in a formal match by the flip of a coin, or in informal play by having whoever is ready to hit first do so. If there are players just ahead of you, it is sometimes customary to let the shortest hitters in your group play first so that you needn't wait as long for the group ahead to be out of range.

When it is your turn, tee your ball between or just behind the markers. If it is a hole with trouble close to the fairway, you may wish to start by driving with your 3 wood rather than with the driver, because the 3 wood is easier to control and also makes it easier to get the ball airborne. Take a practice swing to refresh your muscles' memory. (One or two is adequate—more, a waste of time.) Take a stance so that you are aiming the ball toward the part of the fairway that is farthest from the primary trouble on the hole. Then tell yourself just one thing: "Make your very best swing." There will be a tremendous temptation to *hit* the ball *hard. Treat that first tee shot more like a practice swing*—give your *best* swing, not your hardest.

If you are trying to think of the "hundred" details you learned about swinging—forget them! Just use this key—"swing the club like an uninhibited practice swing"—then go out and have a good time.

PLAYING #1

Well, the first stroke wasn't so bad after all. You had a little slice (a shot that curves to the right; one that curves to the left is called a "hook"), but it stayed in the fairway because you played to the left. It's still a long way to the green. The scorecard says this hole is 410 yards, so you'll need another wood shot. One fellow in the group topped his shot; so after he hits, you can move up to your shot and be ready to go. You remember that these fairway woods should be hit just a little down, like a long iron; so on your practice swing, take a bit of grass to the left of the ball. Practice swing—now real swing the same way—got it in the air, great! Because you didn't catch it quite flush, it won't make the green; but it was a good shot for the first fairway wood. Your friends are looking in the rough (long grass) for a ball, so you should go over and help. The rules say that after five minutes you should declare the ball lost and play another from wherever the ball was hit before it landed in the rough. By the time you join your friends, the ball is found and the players then spread so as not to violate a rule of etiquette by standing too close to and distracting the man who is swinging. His shot out of the rough comes up short of the green and rolls into a greenside hazard (sand trap or bunker). The other two players' balls are on the green, and it's your turn. You select a wedge for the remaining thirty yards. There is a sand trap between you and the pin—your shot must get up into the air. In your eagerness to try to lift the ball, you leave your weight back on the right foot and end up hitting the shot "fat" (behind it), dumping it only eight to ten feet in front of where you are. On the next try, you overcompensate and lift up on the shot (still keeping your weight back instead of to the left) and hit a low screaming shot that flies over the trap and overshoots the green by a good ten yards. The ensuing chip is short of the green by about a yard, and you are tempted to go up and chip again quickly with your wedge just to get on. Instead, you remember that a less-lofted club would be much better here close to the putting surface and therefore switch to your 6 iron while your friend plays from the trap. You notice that when he takes a practice swing he hits the sand—a two-stroke penalty—but apparently he doesn't know the difference. You try to execute your chip shot as though it were a putt because you are only twenty feet from the pin. It comes up just about one and one-half feet from the hole—glad you didn't use your wedge? You must mark your ball—but someone suggests that you just putt out first, which you do successfully. A 7. But you *could* have been putting for a par if you hadn't flubbed that first pitch shot!

THE SECOND HOLE

This hole is a par 5, 515 yards long, and it looks like 515 miles. You'll probably really have to hit hard on this hole. No, wait—that's the wrong way to think. Just three average-length shots with a wood could get you home: 3 × 175 yards would be on the back of the green. That's a better way to think about it. Your partners who had a 5 and a 6 on the first hole retain the honor. You shoot third, and your other companion who also had a 7 is last because he followed you on the first hole. (He didn't count the penalty in the sand. You'll tell him about it when you finish.) You tee your ball up, but in addressing it with your wood you accidentally bump it off the tee. Is that a stroke? One of your more experienced partners tells you it doesn't count because there was no attempt to hit it. He's correct. Your tee shot, this time with the driver, is heeled badly and goes about 120 yards—tried to hit that one too hard! Maybe you'll stay with the 3 wood for a couple more holes.

The last person in your group hits a big slice and exclaims, "Oh, no, O.B.!" After you realize that he means "out-of-bounds," you look up the fairway and notice the white stakes bordering the trees on the right side. Hearing his ball hit in the trees, you start to walk ahead when he says, "Wait, I'll hit a provisional." You recall that a provisional ball is allowed when a player hits a ball that *may* be lost or out-of-bounds. If the ball is in fact out-of-bounds, he plays the provisional and lays 3—a severe penalty for inaccuracy. His next shot is again down the right side but stops just short of the stakes. Had that one gone out, he'd have had to hit another and lie 5. When you reach your ball, you find it is in a poor lie, and you wish you could improve its position as one of the other fellows in the group did on the last hole—but you know it's against the rules. You must play the ball as it lies. This time, however, you use a 3 iron because it seems easier to get it up in the air from that poor lie. You hit the ball thin (almost topped) and leave yourself still a long shot to the green. There is a search going on for the ball in the woods. As you cross the fairway, you notice that the group behind you is coming onto the tee. Mentioning this fact to one of your group, you step out of the trees, whistle, and give them a wave ahead with your arm.

After about a one-minute look, your companion spots a ball back down the fairway a few yards and identifies its make and number as those of the ball that was thought to be out-of-bounds. It turns out to be safe after all. It must have hit the trees and bounced back in. He is ready to play; but since the group behind hasn't quite passed, you must wait. The correct etiquette is to let the group through once you have waved them on. When they reach the green, your friend hits his original ball and lies 2, having abandoned the provisional, which was to be played only if the first one was out-of-bounds. You walk ahead to your shot and decide to use the 3 wood. The green is a little over 200 yards ahead, and the group is still putting; but you will have to hit your best shot to get there, so you just take a nice comfortable swing. You really connect, and it's going right for the players! *Fore!* The players ahead duck as the ball lands just short of the green, climbs the front bank, and rolls between them, then on and over the putting surface. You apologize profusely to them as they leave the green for the third tee. "I didn't know I could hit it that far" sounds a little hollow when you say it; but they accept your statement, probably realizing that you are a beginner.

Behind the green your ball has come to rest right in the base of a bush. There's no way you can hit it. One of your foursome tells you to declare it an *unplayable lie.* So you move the ball two club lengths from the bush (use your driver to measure), going no nearer the hole; stand, holding the ball at arm's length; and drop the ball. Add one penalty stroke, and now you lie 4—still not too bad. You have to clear a large bank to get back on the green, and therefore select your pitching wedge. Your practice swing gives you an idea about how hard you should hit it; but when the actual shot is being played, you become afraid and let up in effort, and the ball fails to clear the bank and comes rolling back down at your feet. The next shot is too hard but fortunately hits the flagstick and drops about six feet from the hole. It would have gone clear over the green except for luck. But wait, is there a penalty for that? Not so, says a companion who anticipates your question. He explains that when you strike the flagstick from off the green, there is no penalty, but striking it from on the green results in a two-stroke penalty.

You must mark your ball because it lies in the path of one of your partners' putts. To mark the ball, you take a small coin from your pocket and place it right at the base of the back of the ball. If the coin had been directly on his line, you could have measured to the right or left with the length of your putter blade and moved it farther from his line. After marking your ball, you take a position behind his line so that you can see which way your putt will break. He steps up to his ball, then backs off and asks you to stand somewhere else since you are standing right along his line within peripheral vision range. He putts. Although he doesn't make it, he continues putting since he is not stepping in anyone's line in taking his stance and he'll move the play along faster. You follow and your ensuing putt stops one foot short of the hole. Your companions say, "Pick it up." This means they will give it to you—conceding that you will certainly make it on your next stroke. This is acceptable in a match play tournament or in an informal game but would not be allowed in formal stroke play competition. It's good practice to hole them all out. Eight for that hole with a penalty stroke! Well, no one ever said it would be easy.

THE THIRD HOLE

You have now moved to the bottom of the batting order with that 8. The fellows that you let through must have been held up because they are just starting to putt on this 145-yard, par 3 hole. But they replace the flag and wave your group on while they stop putting. This practice sometimes saves time on a crowded course by allowing the players following to be walking to the hole after their shots rather than standing while the group on the green is putting. Two in your party hit their shots on the green, while the third is strong, going over the green and onto the next tee area. You catch your shot well with your 7 iron but leave your ball yards short. You thought you would use the same club that the other fellows did, without considering the fact that they normally hit the ball farther than you do. You'll have to learn your own distances for your clubs. You took a big divot on your tee shot. Someone throws it back to you as he starts ahead. You lay the divot back down the way it came out and step on it, knowing that it can grow back.

Because the green has a level approach to it, you elect to use the 7 iron again rather than a high-lofted club, since it seems easier to run the ball when the pin is farther back on the green. It works. You hit a good pitch-and-run shot, which winds up four feet short of the cup. Meanwhile, your partner has found that his ball rolled under the bench on the next tee. It is explained that this is an obstruction that can be moved, so he moves it and hits the ball with no penalty. Had the obstacle been immovable, he could have dropped the ball one club length away from the nearest point of relief (no nearer the hole) also with no penalty. Someone suggests that you learn the difference between "loose impediments," which are natural things like leaves, rocks, and twigs, and obstructions, which are artificial.

Everyone holed their putts, and you are the only one left. The putt breaks a little to the left. You practice the correct effort with a preliminary stroke, step to the ball, and hit it just like your practice swing. It's in! No—it rimmed the cup. Almost a par! You know, you say to yourself, I rather like this game. (Figure 9–1)

Figure 9-1
There's nothing like the joy of success, whether it be over an opponent, the course, or yourself.

By Now You Should Realize That:

Advance reservations are sometimes necessary to play your local course, particularly at peak times.

You should plan to arrive at the course early enough to allow for a suitable warm-up. When on the first tee, you should forget the multitude of details about the swing and just try to picture and feel your very best swing.

The temptation to hit harder on a long shot or long hole should be replaced by the desire to make a good swing in your normal tempo.

There are definite procedures regarding rules, etiquette, and simple logistics of being in the right place at the right time that you should be aware of before venturing on the course.

10

PRACTICE

the way to success

In this chapter you will find:
1. *Motor learning principles.*
2. *Reasons for practicing.*
3. *Ways to practice.*
4. *A form of practice aimed strictly at conditioning you for the game.*

The objective of the first portion of this book was to provide you with enough essential information to enjoy golf your first few times on the course. But as you leave the beginner classification, you'll begin to realize that there is a great deal more to be learned about this game. Problems will face you for which you have no answers. Exposure to playing will create questions that probably did not occur to you at the outset.

You must now go beyond the basic fundamentals. The balance of this volume contains information of interest to people who decide that they are truly going to become golfers, that they are going to invest some time, money, and effort in the game. It is still but a small portion of what could be learned by the enthusiast, but it represents the first step beyond being a beginner golfer.

There is no such thing as a "natural born" golfer. One may have natural ability, but there isn't a fine player in the game of golf today who hasn't spent many hours on the practice tee. The professionals realize that an hour spent in practice can generally reward them with more valuable information about the golf swing than four hours of playing on the course. Practice is an essential ingredient in the formula for golf success. For this reason it deserves the special attention of the serious golf pupil and the more advanced player. After reading this chapter, you may better appreciate why the solitary figure you see out hitting balls on the range when everyone else is playing is often next year's club champion.

Practicing is not all that much of a grind if you approach it correctly. As a matter of fact, some people prefer to practice rather than to play. A professional friend of mine has a sixty-seven-year-old student who hits practice balls by the hour. My friend's comment was, "What is he practicing for? He never plays in any tournaments." But in this case the pro discovered that the gentleman in question simply enjoyed the practice.

It takes a rare individual, however, just to practice for its own sake. You should have something for which to practice. If it is not an upcoming match, tournament, or outing, then your goal should be a certain score on the course or the conquering of a pesky fault. Goal setting crystallizes your practice plans and provides you with a built-in incentive.

Motor Learning Principles

There are certain principles of motor learning with which you should be familiar if you wish to receive maximum returns from your practice efforts:

1. Your emotional state may have a profound effect upon your ability to learn or perfect a skill.

2. Incorrectly practicing a skill will naturally cause retrogression rather than improvement. In other words, practice does not always "make perfect"!

3. Learning may be negatively affected if practice is carried beyond the point of fatigue.

4. For golf it is probably best to work on accuracy and speed simultaneously since both are so essential to the skill. Speed can be sacrificed somewhat, but not to the point at which significant change in the coordinated movement results.

5. Mentally rehearsing the movement may help to accustom you to it.

6. In general, many short practice sessions bring better results than long, widely scattered ones.

WHY PRACTICE?

Show me a golfer who plays the game at par or better, and I will show you a person who has played hundreds of rounds of golf and hit thousands of practice shots. Good golf is not luck or an accident—it is, for one, a great deal of practice. When we speak of "good golf" in this sense, we mean very good golf, par golf. The "good enough just to enjoy it—to heck with the score" level of golf can be attained fairly quickly with some decent instruction and a little practice. (Figure 10–1) But most people have a desire to improve, no matter what level they have reached. It would be grossly unfair and inaccurate even to hint that it is a relatively simple matter to become a truly fine player. Your improvement in this game will be measured in close proportion to the amount of effort you put into it.

Figure 10-1
Starting golf when you are young is a distinct advantage: starting with good instruction makes it even more so.

One of golf's first publicized practicers was a professional named Henry Picard. Picard often had the feeling that he could in one stroke actually hole out shots from 150 yards after an intense practice session. The results he gained by practice showed many other pros the way to much of the improvement we see in scoring today. Picard's greatest influence may have been exerted on one of his young friends, the immortal Ben Hogan. As a fledgling pro, Hogan had been told by several golf teachers that he didn't stand a chance on the tour with *his* golf swing. Picard's encouragement and Hogan's painstaking practice helped Ben make golf history. Since then, the likes of Gary Player, Arnold Palmer, Jack Nicklaus, and Tom Watson have proven the value of dedicated practice.

PRACTICE CORRECTLY

If you practice anything long enough, you can become reasonably automatic in its repetition—bad golf swings included. What a sorry waste of effort it is to see a person practicing and playing with golf fundamentals that make major improvement literally impossible. A man who had been playing golf for a number of years came to me for a lesson. He was very discouraged, to the point of quitting the game, and was skeptical about his chances to improve. But his wife had bought him three private lessons. I have never seen anyone who took such an unorthodox grip on the club; the results could only spell disaster. After three shots I couldn't contain myself and said, "Look, why not just let your arms and hands hang naturally without twisting them into such contortions, and hold on firmly with the last three fingers of your left hand. Then swing the club." (Discounting the grip, the fellow actually had a reasonably good swing.) He tried the correction and produced a shot that, although not spectacular, seemed a miracle to him. "Why, I haven't hit one that good in thirteen years!" he exclaimed. And he meant it. With some additional minor adjustments in his grip, he continued to hit good shots.

The point is, it would have been a complete waste of time for this man to trudge faithfully to the practice tee, dragging along those bad fundamentals. In his case it took only a few minutes to learn something positive and correct on which to practice. After his other two lessons and occasional checkups, he developed a sense of the correct mechanics involved in the preparation and execution of the golf swing. After that he received handsome rewards for the practice time he did spend. You can do likewise if you find yourself a competent teacher, develop an understanding of the basic fundamentals, and decide what you need to practice. Then the time that you do spend practicing will be much more rewarding.

WHERE TO PRACTICE

There are actually several possibilities open to you for a practice site. The most obvious, of course, is the driving range. If you have limited time and can afford it, a driving range can most certainly be a convenient practice facility. In addition to renting balls, they usually provide free clubs, are sometimes covered to protect you from rain, and are occasionally heated in cold weather.

Or you can look for some nearby open space where you could hit practice balls without endangering anyone: a remote area of a park, an unused playing field, an area bordering the golf course, the beach, or any place that has short or no grass and an absence of people. If you find such a spot, then buy some used balls from the golf course or use your old ones that have become unfit for play but are acceptable for practice. Purchase a shag bag (one used for holding practice balls) or obtain an old airline flight bag, bowling ball container, or overnight case in which to keep your practice ball supply. Owning your own practice balls is a strong incentive to practice if you can find a place to use them.

Not all practice needs to be done out-of-doors or with real balls. One alternative to the driving range and the open field is the indoor net.

A great deal can be learned about the swing when made indoors where the golfer is concerned not about the flight of the ball but rather the feeling of the swing. Some fine players have been developed at indoor winter golf schools where the motto was, "The swing's the thing."

HOW TO PRACTICE

Driving ranges should be renamed. The title encourages people to hit shots exclusively with their drivers, as if it were the only club in their bag. Most of these people are trying to see how far they can propel the ball. This really isn't practice—it's just an expensive form of exercise. Any relationship between that kind of practice and score improvement is purely coincidental. If we started calling these areas "practice ranges" or "learning centers" rather than driving ranges, we might be on the right track. Besides a good deal of your practice should be spent on the shots around the green. (Figure 10–2)

What you should be trying to develop in any practice session in which you are working on your swing is a feeling that is comfortable and repeatable—one that you could repeat a thousand times the same way if you had to. To acquire that feeling, first employ a warm-up that consists of swinging two or even three clubs at a time. The added resistance provided by the extra club or clubs slows your tempo and, because of the

Figure 10-2
Practice on the short game can reduce scores faster than any other use of time.

added weight, makes you more aware of the centrifugal force. After you have completed this warm-up, start hitting shots with your short clubs and work up gradually to the woods. When you get to your driver, be just as concerned with accuracy and rhythm as you were with your irons. With all of that open space in front of you, there is an almost uncontrollable urge to just "let it fly" drive after drive. If you succumb to this temptation, you will find yourself overswinging and losing the repeatable controlled feeling that you have been trying to build. Treat your tee shot swing much like the swings for the rest of your clubs. A former U.S. Open champion once remarked that he never consciously tries to hit a long drive. Nonetheless, he undeniably hits many.

As much as possible, make your practice sessions simulate the real game. Hit from the grass when possible; use a target on all your shots; alternate the clubs, sometimes going from a wood to a short iron as you would in the playing of a hole; imagine that you are playing a particular shot on a hole at your home course; then watch the result.

If you will apply these practice tips to the fine instruction that is available to you through books, professional teachers, and school instructors, better scores will soon be coming your way.

CONDITIONING YOUR BODY

It is fairly obvious that practicing by hitting golf balls and swinging will help you improve. But there are other kinds of practice related to the game that may be of value. The question arises: Will you play better golf if you are stronger and in better plysical condition? Will certain exercises improve your game? The honest answer is that no one really knows because this subject has not been researched thoroughly. But from my experience, I would emphatically say, "Yes!" The right exercises given to the right people for the right reasons can, I'm convinced, help one's golf.

Most right-handed golfers, for example, are weak in the left arm and hand. Some are so weak that they are prone to the following mistakes: letting loose of the club with the last three fingers of the left hand at the top of the backswing; bending the left arm; failing to pull strongly with the left side. All of these fundamental errors in the swing could probably be helped simply by strengthening the left side.

I conducted a laboratory study that supported that importance of strength in driving a golf ball for distance. Distance, although important to golf, is, of course, not the complete game. However, since longer drives do correlate with lower scoring, it is logical to assume that strength plays some role in good golf.

Strength alone is not the only physical factor that influences the distance picture. In fact, for some, flexibility and timing may be more important. When you consider the many factors that affect this one aspect of golf—driving—and then add the other parts of the game, such as chipping and putting, attitude, and experience, you realize the difficulty with saying that such and such an exercise will make you play better golf. But certainly the stronger, more flexible player possesses greater potential to score.

Some of the exercise suggestions that are supposed to help your golf have ranged from simply making a fist to doing one-hand extension push-ups on the finger tips. In the former case, anyone could do it; in the latter, probably one person in 50,000 could. I seriously doubt if either of these suggestions for increasing strength would help your golf more than any of a hundred other types of exercises.

I am firmly convinced that a lack of general body conditioning can be a handicap to a person hoping to play good golf. (Figures 10-3, 10-4, 10-5) In my earlier study on the drive for distance, the evidence clearly indicated that increasing age was accompanied by increasing physical deterioration and decreasing ability to hit a long golf drive. To what extent physical deterioration or lack of fitness affects the rest of the golf game is still a matter of conjecture.

It is reasonable also to assume that fatigue can have an effect upon a skill like golf, which requires such a high degree of precision. If this is the case, then a person highly conditioned for endurance activities will be better able to ward off the prospect of deteriorating play due to fatigue.

Without knowing your case specifically, it would be difficult to

Figure 10-3
My own strength training includes work on a Distance Builder.

Figure 10-4
Gym-in-a-Bag, also for strength.

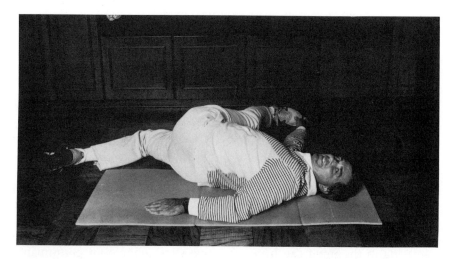

Figure 10-5
Flexibility exercises are very important if you tend to be tight or as you get older.

prescribe the best type of exercise program for your golf game. In my book *Super-Power Golf* (Contemporary, 1984), a complete training program for increased distance is offered. Briefly, what appears to be a most sensible and economical approach to the problem of conditioning your body for golf is this:

1. Any program that improves your overall strength, flexibility, and endurance will probably help.

2. Using the principle of overload (or moving increased weight through the same motions you make in a golf swing) seems sound. You might take an object heavier than a normal golf club—such as a weighted club, bar from a barbell, rake, or homemade weighted device—and swing it like your golf club.

3. If you use weights, concentrate on the legs, forearms, back, and hands, while deemphasizing the biceps, upper shoulders, and chest. (Heavy development in the latter areas restricts your swing.)

4. Be sure to include walking, jogging, running, or skipping rope—something that works your legs and builds endurance.

5. Do sit-ups and other lower-back exercises and work on a good stretching program. This will help strengthen your back and protect you from the problems that ail even the tour players.

CONDITIONING YOUR MIND

The term "psychosomatic" is generally applied to illnesses that are induced or nurtured by a psychic cause. Those psychic forces that we think can actually work against us physically can also be turned around to work for us. Book titles like *The Power of Positive Thinking, You Can Work Your Own Miracles,* and *Powers of Mind* suggest the positive approach to a sort of psychosomatics in reverse of its usual context.

You should begin to condition your mind in a positive way before you even get to the golf course. Research studies have clearly demonstrated that a form of mental practice, that is, spending some quiet time thinking of a physical task, such as shooting a free throw, making a dive or a downhill ski run, or performing a gymnastics stunt, can be *as* effective as and sometimes *more* effective than the same amount of time spent in actual physical practice. Of course, there are some conditions to this, including the matter of proper technique; but it has been demonstrated that mental practice can be a useful aid in learning physical skills.

Mental practice in the form of positive visualization as a way to improve your swing has been suggested in the golf literature from as far back as fifty years ago. A bit more recently (1978), in a book I co-authored with Dr. Richard Coop called *The New Golf Mind* (Simon & Schuster), we detail the broad extent to which the mind affects shot making. This imaging in the mind can have a positive effect upon your performance and is indeed worth your attention.

Some type of mental visualization is practiced by the touring

Figure 10-6
Watching Tour players perform can be a great learning experience in creating positive mental imagery.

professionals consistently *during* their play. For example, one player may try to visualize his swing for the next shot while he is walking toward it. While putting, players may try to see the ball actually proceed along the intended line and drop into the hole before they putt. Others try to do the same with their short shots around the green, mentally picturing the anticipated trajectory and noting where the ball will land and how it will roll, before they even step up to make the shot. Players will also picture the techniques of other particularly good performers. (Figure 10–6) This technique is so widely practiced that it is hard to discount the fact that it is effective. Unquestionably, it is an important part of the game.

You Should Have Learned that Your Golf Game Depends upon the Realization that:

There is no "easy way" to become a proficient golfer. Practice is one of the essential ingredients to make progress toward that goal.

Practice alone, without a knowledge of the proper mechanics, is an inefficient expenditure of time and energy.

Worthwhile alternatives to practicing at the driving range are using a net, swinging in the backyard, using available open space, and practicing mentally.

The practice sessions in which you are working on the full swing should be devoted to developing a consistently repeatable stroke.

Physical conditioning and mental practice are two extra types of work routines that will help your game.

11

CORRECTING GOLF'S
MOST FREQUENT ERRORS

the errors most often made

Because everyone hits bad shots, you now need to know:
1. What causes these shots.
2. How to make the fundamental corrections.

One of the first things you learn when hitting a golf ball is that all the shots don't go where you want them to. In fact, more of them deviate from the intended line than stay on it. Improvement in the game comes through decreasing the percentage of shots that falls into this latter category. The four most common "bad" shots are the topped shot, the fat shot, the slice, and the hook.

Even the greatest golfers hit these bad shots at times. But the difference between the fine player and the poor one is that the fine player doesn't hit them as often, and when he does, he knows how to correct them. The poor player will chronically repeat the error over and over, season after season, frequently for his whole golfing lifetime. This form of self-torture is quite unnecessary since there are cures for all known golf "diseases."

Even when you know the causes and cures for golf ailments, it is sometimes difficult to make the right correction. Obviously, the touring professionals whose livelihoods depend upon being able to make good golf swings know their swings in detail. But even pros have their pros to whom they go when in trouble. The reason is that we often can't feel or see in ourselves the mistakes that we are making. It frequently takes someone with a trained and objective eye to spot our problems. Be extremely careful, however, about taking advice from well-meaning "semi-pros." If you encourage it, and sometimes even if you don't, you may be deluged with tips on curing your current golf ailments. A friend or even a complete stranger may try to force on you a pet cure that worked for him one time. More than likely it is a compensation for another error of his and may be totally unrelated to your basic problem. You'll save yourself much money, time, and frustration if you politely reply that you are going to have a lesson the next day with the professional to have the problem taken care of. Then, *do it!*

TOPPING

If you have watched much golf, you know that in all cases, except putting, a successfully executed golf shot travels in the air. Those that bound along the ground are considered undesirable. It is probably this urge to get the ball "up" that causes people to try and scoop it or lift it into the air. In previous chapters you have learned that the clubface is built with loft that will elevate the ball if you just deliver the clubface on the ball. To help you to swing slightly down through the shot, you should develop a foot-work pattern that concludes the swing with a positive weight transfer to the left. (Figure 11–1) People who try to scoop the ball *up* generally finish the swing either flat-footed or with their weight back on their right sides. Three key words can help a person overcome this serious fault: *left, down,* and *through.* Think of those three keys, in that order, before you swing. Say to yourself: "I must shift my weight to the *left* while pulling with my *left* arm, and try to feel as though I am swinging the club a little bit *down.* I will continue that motion *through* to a good finish." By programming your thoughts in this way and using the following tips, you should not have further problems topping the ball.

Figure 11-1
On a full swing always finish with your weight fully to the left and your right foot on the toe.

Figure 11-2
The left arm has collapsed because the right is tight and trying to lift the ball. The result is a topped shot.

1. Take a practice swing that takes a slight divot of grass in front or to the left of the ball. Try to do the same thing when you get to the shot. This demonstrates your correct transfer of weight to the left.

2. The right hand is the culprit that tries to scoop the shot and results in pulling you up in the air, away from the ball. Be more conscious of using your left side to pull down toward the ball. Actively using the left arm helps keep it in the desirable extended position. (Figure 11-2)

3. Check to see that you are not reaching too far for the ball; rather, your arms should hang comfortably after you have bent from the hips.

Other causes of topping—like trying to hit too hard, bending your left elbow, and picking your head up—are related to not getting to the left and not using your left side properly so that it arrives in proper sequence, before the clubhead.

SCLAFFING (HITTING THE SHOT FAT)

"Sclaffing" means hitting behind the ball, displacing a lot of earth but moving the ball only a short distance. It is a first cousin to topping in that the causes and cures are almost the same. If you frequently hit behind the ball, check the following:

1. Are you trying to hit the ball before you have transferred your weight to the left foot? An early release of power by prematurely uncocking the hands can cause the shocking experience of contacting the earth before the ball, much to the displeasure of your wrists. Unfortunately, this often discourages people from doing the very thing they should be doing: hitting slightly down through the shot. Again, you need to emphasize the lead of the left side and the transfer of weight. This will help you get your swing sequence in order.

2. You may have placed the ball too far forward in your stance so that the bottom of the arc of your swing is falling at the correct spot but the ball isn't there to be hit. Check your practice swing to see that the ball is played so that its front side corresponds to the point where your divot mark begins.

3. Check to see that you haven't gotten too close to the ball in your address. Your arms should be in an extended hanging position. The arms will tend to extend naturally during the correct swing. If they are bent at address, the club may not have room to clear the ground. But standing too far away is more of a problem than standing too close.

4. Lowering your head or swing center during the swing could also cause you to make your initial contact with the ground rather than with the ball, though it is a less common reason.

SLICING

Once a person has learned to get the ball into the air, the slice (a shot curving from left to right) is by far the biggest problem he will likely face. It is the nemesis of thousands of golfers, many of whom have come to believe that it can't be cured. This, of course, is ridiculous. Anyone can learn to hit the ball without producing a slice.

One of the main reasons for a mass-population golf disease like the slice is that the body and hand positions in the swing that encourage a slice are more comfortable and more instinctive than those that produce the straight shot. Man usually seeks the way of least resistance in everything he does; golf seems to be no exception. The slice was also, in a sense, inadvertently built into the older methods of teaching, which in some quarters still persist. By "built in" I mean that the accepted technique of rolling the face open and then trying to close it during the swing requires the player to have excellent timing plus strong and supple wrists before the slice disappears. Unfortunately, a great number of people are simply unable to correct their weakness. And so the slice remains a prevalent error plaguing the average golfer. Here are some basic clues for curing that dreaded shot.

1. A slice is caused by hitting the ball with the face open to the line on which you are swinging. This can happen when, 1) the face is square to the target but the swing is traveling to the left, that is, outside

to in, or 2) when the path is correct but the face is open, looking to the right of the path. (Figure 11–3) Any correction you make applying to a slice should work toward alleviating one or both of these faults.

2. Check your swing line first. Put a club down along your line of flight and see if the swing "feels" like it is traveling from the inside of that line slightly out and then on toward the target. In actual fact, to hit the ball straight the club must approach the ball from inside the flight line and then go directly on the line toward the target before continuing around into the follow-through. It will feel as though the clubhead is coming from inside the line of flight and continuing out slightly to the right of the target before finishing the swing. If you find that you are crossing the line of flight before striking the ball (hitting from the outside in), then make the following corrections:

Get your swing back in sequence, which basically is (a) weight back to the left side, (b) arms swinging down and forward as hips turn to the target, and (c) hands releasing the power by forearm rotation and uncocking of the wrists. When the hands start to release ahead of the weight shift and arm swing, the club is thrown outside the flight line, cutting across that intended path. When the face fails to match that path and stays open to it, a slice is produced. By getting the swing back in sequence with the forearms and hands releasing later in the downswing, you will approach the ball from inside the intended flight line rather than outside. One other element you have to look for is the alignment of your body in relation to your intended line. Most important is your shoulder line, as it has the strongest influence on swing path. If your shoulders point to the left, they encourage your swing to go that way. The hips and feet influence

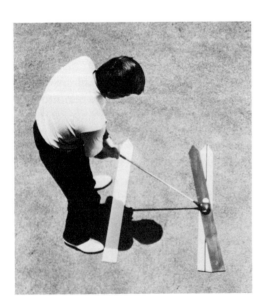

Figure 11-3
The shoulders are aiming left, which encourages the swing path to travel the dark arrow across your intended path. When the face is square to your intended line but open to your swing path it applies a "cutting action" or sidespin to the ball making it slice.

the shoulders and therefore should be considered. Basically, an open stance, or one with the left foot pulled back from the line of flight, encourages slicing by helping to produce an outside-to-in swing path. So get your body alignment correct and your sequences in order. Then the path will be correct.

3. If your swing is already coming from the inside or if you have just worked on this fundamental and are still slicing, then you have one more place to look—the clubface. In order to square it, take a strong grip with your left hand (that means three knuckles on the back of your hand showing). Swing the clubhead away in a square position for the first ten to twelve inches, square rather than turning the toe open (to the right). At the top of your swing, when your wrists are cocked, make certain that the back of your left hand and your wrist are at least in a straight line, and possibly even in a slightly convex position. If instead the left wrist is cupped so that wrinkles appear under the wrist joint rather than beneath the thumb, the face of the club is probably open and the back of your left hand should be flattened to the level of the forearm. When you enter the hitting area on the downswing, try to see that the back of your hand is facing the target rather than looking up at you. You may at first have to forcibly close the face with your left hand by turning the toe of your club over in a counterclockwise rotation. Make certain that the clubhead is traveling toward the target. After a few attempts, it should become more natural rather than forced. Let your forearm rotate and release the clubhead to come over and through the shot. Feel the weight of the clubhead! If your wrists feel stiff, you haven't made a complete release. Should you start hooking the ball severely, work the left-hand grip back to two knuckles. These aids will work if you do them. I've had people working on their slice with these techniques who said, "It doesn't work." But when I watched them perform, I had to tell them, "It didn't work because you didn't do it." You may sometimes feel as though you are doing what you are supposed to; but if the ball does not react correctly, obviously, then, you are not.

HOOKING

It has often been said that good golfers are more likely to hook rather than to slice. The only thing good about a hook is that it may indicate a certain strength in the hands and wrists of the beginner, assets that are later quite helpful in becoming an accomplished player. An uncontrolled hook can get you into just as much trouble, if not more, as a slice. Its only advantage is that it generally will produce more distance than a slice because it has less backspin. The causes and cures for this shot are just about the reverse of those for the slice.

To hook a ball, you must either have the face closed to the intended path or hit it markedly from inside out with the face square. It is impossible to hook a ball in any other way. Unlike the slice, it is much harder to hit the ball from an exaggerated inside-out position, and so this fault is much less common. Here are some sources of error.

1. Look first to your grip. If either hand is turned too far to the right (clockwise) on the grip, so that the "V's" are pointing outside your right shoulder, move them more on top of the shaft. Adjust them together. Most commonly, the right hand is placed too far under the shaft.

2. If your grip appears to be correct, then look at the top of your backswing to see if you have hooded (closed) the clubface. If the face of your club is pointing directly to the sky, it is closed. The result will most likely be a sharp hook. An arched (opposite to cupped) left wrist will cause the hooding; therefore, flatten your left wrist instead of letting it fold toward the inside of your forearm.

3. Finally, the most common source of the hooked shot is letting your right hand overpower your left during the swing. If the left arm quits or doesn't do its share, the force of the right hand will close the face of the club and hook the ball. To keep this from happening, take a firmer grip with the last three fingers of your left hand and maintain the grip you started with in your right. It is quite common to change or regrip in the right hand during the swing. You have much less chance of hooking if your right-hand grip is correctly made in the fingers rather than in the palm and fingers. Finally, use your left arm aggressively in the swing so that the right doesn't catch up too soon and collapse the left, causing the swing path to go left.

UNEVEN LIES: A CAUSE FOR BAD SHOTS

One of the factors that can encourage a golfer to hit a shot that is topped, sclaffed, hooked, or sliced is finding his ball lying on uneven terrain—a common experience on most courses. By making adjustments in your stance and alignment, you can combat these tendencies to err. Study the following situations and become familiar with the correct adjustments (see Figure 11–4). For a more complete treatment of the problems we face in playing the game and how they can be handled, refer to *Golf's Common Errors and How to Correct Them* by Gary Wiren with Dawson Taylor, published by Contemporary.

As You Correct Your Shots, You Should Remember That:

The techniques for curing the topped shot and fat shot are often the same.

Slicing is caused by hitting the ball with an open face, by cutting across the intended line of flight from outside in, or a combination of both.

If you are swinging correctly by approaching the ball from inside

A. Ball above your feet.

When the ball is above your feet, the tendency is to pull or hook to the left.

To adjust, simply aim more to the right of the target. Also check to see that your club can clear the ground in a practice swing. Take one club stronger than usual for the distance and swing comfortably. Gravity will try to pull you backward, particularly on a hard swing.

B. Ball below your feet.

When the ball is below your feet the tendency is to push the ball or slice.

To adjust, simply aim more to the left of your target. Make sure that you are standing close enough to the ball that you won't top it, and make a special effort to stay down with the shot. Let your weight be more to the heels and sitting, since gravity wants to pull you forward.

C. Uphill lie.

In an uphill lie, the tendency is to pull the ball and hit short of your target.

To adjust, use at least one club stronger than usual for the distance and possibly more if the grade is severe. Keep your weight to the left side and play the ball a little farther in your stance. Aim slightly to the right. Fight gravity by working up the hill to the left in the swing.

In a downhill lie, the tendency is to fade the shot to the right and to skull or top it.

To adjust, aim to the left and let the ball fade. Play the ball slightly back of center in your stance and stay down with the shot, following the contour of the ground. Level your shoulders more to the slope of the ground.

D. Downhill lie.

Figure 11–4
Uneven lies.

your intended line of flight and are still slicing, then work on closing the face by strengthening the position of your grip, flattening your wrist at the top of your swing, or getting more aggressive hand action and forearm rotation.

The most common cause of the hook is a dominant right hand caused by an improper grip.

You should seek advice from a competent golf professional if you are unable to cure your golfing errors.

12

WHAT SCIENCE CAN TELL US ABOUT GOLF

sorting fact from fiction

This chapter aims to:
1. Relate the facts known about the game that are based on scientific evidence.
2. Apply these facts, in a final mechanical analysis, to that elusive skill known as the golf swing.

The body of knowledge that has been developed around the game of golf in the last 500 years is largely empirical—the result of personal observation and experience. Teaching methods and playing techniques have evolved as an art rather than a science. Golf has, for the most part, eluded the onrush of scientific investigation. But the "unscientific" approach to problem solving, even in golf, is largely a thing of the past. The modern golfer is intelligent enough to insist on knowing the "why" of the golf swing in addition to the "how." The research that has been performed in the area of golf has supported, to a large extent, the practices of current teaching professionals. In some cases, however, traditional thinking has been directly challenged, and a need for some rethinking on several points has developed.

THE BRITISH GOLF STUDIES

By far the most complete scientific investigation yet completed on golf was the research work sponsored some time ago (material published in 1963) by the Golf Society of Great Britain. Spearheaded by a wealthy real estate investor, Sir Aynsley Bridgland, the society attracted some of the finest researchers in the British Isles. Their disciplines included medicine, anatomy, biomechanics, physiology, physical education, ergonomics, ballistics, physics, and engineering. Some of their findings are presented in

The Search for the Perfect Swing by Cochran and Stobbs (1968). The following are some highlights from their work.

Equipment

A drive that carries 200 yards in the air when the ball is at 71 degrees Fahrenheit will carry only 185 yards at 32 degrees. This supports the practice of changing balls at each hole in cold weather and substituting one that has been warming in the player's back pocket from body heat. (Artificial warmers for golf balls are not legal in competition.)

The best combination of club weight to produce maximum distance can be determined only by personal experience in hitting balls. A longer-shafted driver (up to about four inches over the standard forty-three inches for men), however, would give one an advantage in distance without significant loss of accuracy.

Putters weighted at both the toe and the heel have less chance of hitting errant putts when they strike the ball an off-center blow.

The speed of the greens one plays may dictate the best weight of putter to choose.

Equipment can be specially manufactured to reduce a player's tendency to slice, hook, top, or whatever.

The Full Swing

The legs and trunk must play a greater part in producing distance for the top-class player than the arms and hands, since some thirty pounds of muscle is necessary to generate clubhead speed of around 100 miles per hour. (Figure 12–1)

The ball is from fifteen to twenty yards down the fairway before the player has a chance to react to what he felt at impact.

Although the left-arm swing alone is truly representative of the mechanics of a model golf swing, it can produce only three-quarters of the distance of a properly timed two-handed hit.

The difference between a well-timed hit and a poorly timed hit is only about one-fiftieth of a second.

A one-degree error in the clubface aim at impact will result in approximately an 8-yard error by the time the ball carries 200 yards.

The clubhead is moving its fastest during the swing at a point just before it catches up with the hands.

Putting and Chipping

The right hand for right-handed players seems to have greater sensitivity and therefore is important in developing touch for the short game.

The ball is on the putter face for a long putt about the same length of time as for a drive (roughly one-half millisecond).

Figure 12-1
Tour star Tom Watson has developed a business-like, no frills type golf swing which utilizes the legs and trunk to good advantage and generates a swing speed of around 116 m.p.h.

Deliberate efforts to import topspin or backspin to a putt are of insignificant value.

Even a perfect putting machine was able to hole only 50 percent of its putts from a twenty-foot distance owing to irregularities even on a good putting surface.

APPLYING SCIENCE TO THE SWING

Science usually deals with details. Trying to think of details during a golf swing, particularly as a new player, can be ruinous. Therefore, the earlier description of the golf swing in this book was based largely on feel rather than on detail. At this point it may be worthwhile to explain the details behind the feelings.

The golf swing takes approximately two seconds to complete. In that time it is humanly impossible to consider in sequential order the physical details of what is or should be happening. Those people who try to think their way through the swing fail miserably. It is important, however, to be knowledgeable concerning certain details of the swing and to understand it from a purely mechanical standpoint. Without this understanding you will find it difficult to make sound adjustments and corrections when your swing goes sour.

The objective of a full swing is to deliver the clubface in such a way that the ball travels on the intended line of flight and carries the correct distance. Now, there would be no real problem of hitting a ball straight if you needed to move it only a few yards. Evidence the short putt, which is rarely missed in direction by more than a matter of inches. But in the full golf shot, the need for distance complicates the problem of accuracy. For example, in order to make the ball travel far enough to get to a par 4 green in two shots, you must generate considerable clubhead speed and deliver it squarely to the ball. A physical law that is essential to developing that speed is centrifugal force. Applied to the golf swing, it is the force that tends to impel the clubhead outward from the center of rotation. This outward "pulling" action helps the swing attain its maximum arc, thereby providing it with the greatest potential for speed. Given the same rotational force, then, the wider the arc, the greater the speed. This fact theoretically gives taller people with long arms an advantage in achieving distance. You could create a similar increase in mechanical advantage with longer clubs. It doesn't guarantee distance, however, because a tall person or someone with an extra long club may not be able to generate much rotational force or to deliver an accurate blow. Nonetheless, this information concerning the importance of attaining a wide arc should cause people to consider both their equipment and their techniques.

It is to this feature, a wide arc, that the PGA Tour's present longest driver, Davis Love, III, attributes his incredible distance. The value of an extended left arm, particularly through the hitting area, then becomes more apparent. This longer lever simply has more potential for producing force. It should be maintained in an extended position throughout the backswing because it is more efficient and conducive to consistency than bending the elbow and then trying to return the arm to the ball extended again.

The length of the backswing can also affect the potential velocity. A longer swing will involve more muscles and give the player more time to build up speed. Diminishing returns usually occur when, on the backswing, the club drops below a level parallel with the ground. At this point additional force is needed to overcome gravity in bringing the club back up; and, more important, the player generally loses the control that is necessary to make solid contact with the ball.

Another scientifically based principle in the swing is observed in the momentum that is developed in the clubhead on the downswing. When the left arm reaches a point approximately forty-five degrees from a vertical line running through the ball, the wrists and hands begin to make their contribution to the summation of forces that was initiated by the hips and followed by the shoulders and arms. Not until the left arm reaches a point less than ten degrees from vertical should the wrists allow their final bit of energy to be released. This is known as the "delayed hit." It represents the maximum in efficiency of power in the golf stroke because it succeeds in blending the forces of trunk, arms, and hands in a flowing motion of power. The delayed hit builds its speed by one force contributing its effort just as the other force is beginning to diminish (see Figure 12–2). This gradual building of force and speed in its most efficient progression is known as "timing." Its presence can be observed in a well-executed football pass, baseball throw, or javelin hurl. The sequence of lever action is essentially the same—hip rotation, arm and shoulder action, with the wrists and hands coming in last.

The follow-through is only an indication of what went on before. An abbreviated follow-through is a strong sign that clubhead speed was diminishing before the ball was ever struck. It suggests a hitting-*at* movement rather than a hitting-*through* action. An artificial continuation of the swing for form's sake after its energy has been spent is worthless. But if the natural pulling action developed by the club's velocity carries through to a strong, full finish, you probably have maintained your maximum clubhead speed in the hitting zone. In that case a good finish means something.

With such a forceful swing (traveling over 100 miles per hour), it is necessary to have a strong base of support. Too wide a stance affects the rotational range of your trunk and shoulders, while too narrow a stance

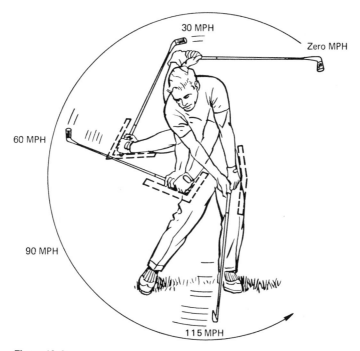

Figure 12–2
The delayed hit. Speeds indicated are arbitrary values approximating the speed of a strong player's swing.

does not give you adequate equilibrium for such a powerful effort. A stance of approximately hip width is conducive to the best mechanics for a full swing for distance.

Owing to the importance of having to make a lateral shift toward the target, you need adequate footing. With friction alone, it is difficult to maintain the foot's stability against such a force. Golf spikes are needed. Without the added traction offered by cleated shoes, the feet may slip and cause a loss of both power and accuracy. If you have ever tried to throw a ball and had your back foot slip just as you were applying your drive off that foot, you may understand what is meant.

The mechanics of golf are difficult to perform consistently because you are dealing with a striking instrument much longer than those used in other sports and one that is traveling at much higher speeds. In addition, once the club is delivered, it has a comparatively small hitting surface that must strike the ball squarely to achieve a satisfactory result. These factors alone make it clear why it takes considerable time to master consistency in hitting a golf ball. On the other hand, a golf ball is sitting still. It does not require the same hand-eye coordination or highly sensitive reaction time as does a sport like baseball or tennis. Also, the adjustment for height is built into the equipment. It requires the player to exercise only preliminary deliberative-type judgment, not split-second adjustment. If it were not for these latter factors, golf would be too hard to play. As it is, the game is stimulating, but not impossible. I hope that you are up to the challenge.

AFTER READING THIS CHAPTER, YOU SHOULD KNOW THAT:

Equipment design and material can have a definite effect upon the results you get when striking a golf ball.

The margin of error in golf between a good and a poor shot is very small.

Understanding the mechanical principles involved in making a golf swing should help you to make sound adjustments in your game.

A longer lever, either in the arm or in the length of club, has a potential for greater force in the swing.

The follow-through in golf is simply an indication of the quality of the swing that preceded it.

The summation of the physical forces of the body in a well-timed sequence and employed in the golf swing is known as the "delayed hit."

You can indeed become proficient at the game of golf if you want to.

THE LANGUAGE OF GOLF

Ace: A hole completed in one stroke.

Address: The process that a player goes through in positioning himself and the club for the stroke.

Approach shot: A full stroke played to the putting green, usually made with a medium or short iron.

Apron: The bordering grass around the green, not as short as the green but usually shorter than the fairway. Sometimes called the "fringe" or "froghair."

Away: The ball deemed farthest from the hole and to be played first.

Best ball: A type of play in which the lower score of either of two partners is counted in the match.

Birdie: One stroke less than the par for the hole.

Bite: Backspin imparted to the ball, which makes it stop abruptly.

Bogey: One stroke more than the par for the hole.

Break of green: The slant or the slope of the green, sometimes called "borrow," when considering the amount of curve to allow for.

Bunker: A hazard in the fairway or rough or near the green, which may take the form of a mound or depression and can be filled with grass or sand. The term is often used synonymously with "sand trap."

Caddy: A person who carries a player's clubs and otherwise assists him in play in accordance with the rules.

Callaway system: A method of handicapping players who have no established handicaps by applying the score a player has just made to a predetermined formula; used particularly in one-day outings for infrequent golfers.

Carry: The distance that a ball travels in the air before striking the ground.

Casual water: A temporary accumulation of water that is not meant to be played as a hazard.

Chip shot: A short and usually low-trajectory shot played to the green.

Closed clubface: One in which the face of the club points to the left of the intended line of flight.

Closed stance: A position of the feet in which the right foot is withdrawn from an imaginary line across the toes that runs parallel to the line of flight.

Cocked: A position of the wrists in which the left wrist is laterally flexed (toward thumb side) and the right wrist is dorsally hinged (back of hand toward forearm).

Divot: A piece of sod taken from the ground by a player's stroke, which should be replaced and stamped down.

Dogleg: A bend in the fairway that crooks similarly to the hind leg of a dog.

Dormie: A player or side that is ahead in a match by as many holes as there are left to play; used only in match play competition.

Double bogey: Two over the par for the hole.

Double eagle: Three under the par for the hole or, most commonly, a score of 2 on a par 5 hole; also called an "albatross."

Down: The number of holes or strokes that a player is behind his opponent.

Draw: A shot that curves slightly from right to left; slight hook.

Driver: The number 1 wood club that is most often used from the teeing area.

Dub: A poor golfer or a poorly hit shot.

Duffer: A player with poor skills.

Eagle: Two strokes under the par for the hole.

Explosion shot: A forceful shot made in a sand trap, which displaces a large amount of sand and forces the ball upward and out of the trap.

Fade: A shot that curves in flight slightly from left to right.

Fairway: That portion of grass between the tee and green that is kept well mowed so as to provide the ball a good lie.

Fat shot: A swing in which the clubhead strikes the ground before the ball and thereby decreases the distance of the shot; also called "sclaffing."

Flag or flagstick: A marker placed on the green, indicating the location of the cup.

Flat swing: A technique of swinging that employs a less vertical and more horizontal swing than normal. The backswing may stay below shoulder level.

Flight: The path that the ball takes in the air; or a division of players in a tournament according to playing ability.

Follow-through: The remainder of the swing after the ball has been hit.

Fore!:   A warning cry to anyone who stands in danger of being hit by a ball.

Foursome: Four players playing together in a group. It technically means two players playing against two others, but with each side playing only one ball between them, hitting alternate shots.

Grain: The direction that the grass grows and lies on the putting green. It can have a marked effect on both the break and the distance allowed for in a putt.

Gross score: The actual number of strokes a player has taken before his handicap is deducted.

Halved: A hole that each player or side in match play competition has played in the same number of strokes. It means a tie, or one-half a hole for one side with one-half a hole for the other.

Handicap: A rating of a player's ability relative to shooting par; used to equalize competition between players of unequal ability.

Hazard: In general use, any natural obstacles on the course, such as trees, ponds, ditches, bunkers, etc., but more specifically, by rule, bunkers and water hazards.

Heeled shot: A shot hit near or off the portion of the club that attaches to the shaft.

Hole high: Ball that has come to rest even with the hole but off to one side.

Hole out: To complete the play of the hole by hitting the ball into the cup.

Honor: The right to drive or play first from the teeing ground; determined by the lowest score on the previous hole or on the first tee by the flip of a coin.

Hook: A golf shot that curves from right to left. A "duck hook" or "smothered hook" would be one that is particularly low to the ground and curves sharply to the left.

Lie: The position in which the ball has come to rest on the ground; or the angle that the shaft makes with the ground when the club is properly soled.

Links: Originally a seaside golf course, but now used frequently to mean any course.

Loft of the club: The amount or degree of pitch that is built into the clubface.

Loose impediments: Natural objects that are not fixed or growing, such as twigs, loose rocks, pine cones, leaves.

Match play: A form of golf competition in which each hole is a separate contest. The winner is determined by holes won rather than total score.

Medalist: The player who has shot the lowest qualifying round for a tournament; also, the player with the lowest score in a team match.

Medal play or stroke play: A form of golf competition in which the winner is determined by the lowest score for the round. The rules of golf differ slightly between match and medal play.

Mixed foursome: A group of four players made up of two men and two women.

Mulligan: The common but illegal practice of driving an extra ball on the first hole in the event that the original ball is not to the player's liking.

Nassau: A method of scoring a match based upon the allowance of three points: one for the winner of each nine and one for the winner of the total eighteen holes.

Net score: A player's score after having subtracted his handicap from his gross, or actual, score.

Obstruction: Anything artificial or man-made, whether erected, placed, or left on the course, except objects defining the course boundaries, such as stakes, fences, or walls; also, artificially constructed roadways or pathways.

Open stance: A position of the feet in which the left foot is withdrawn from an imaginary line across the toes that runs parallel to the line of flight.

Open tournament: One in which both professionals and amateurs can compete together.

Out-of-bounds: Any area outside the boundaries of the course as defined by white stakes or some other designated marker.

Par: A theoretical score representing a standard of excellence based upon the length of the hole and allowing for two putts.

Penalty stroke: A stroke added to a player's score for an infraction of the rules.

Pitch shot: A short lofted shot made with the intention of getting the ball onto the green.

Press: To attempt to hit the ball harder than usual; or to double a previously made bet in a game for stakes by initiating a new and second game from the time of the press to the end of the nine holes being played.

Provisional ball: An extra ball that is hit when a player feels that his original ball may be lost or out-of-bounds.

Pulled shot: Shot that travels to the left of the intended line.

Pushed shot: Shot that travels to the right of the intended line.

Rough: The long grass and other vegetation that border the fairway and surround the green.

Rub-of-the-green: The occurrence of a ball that is in motion being stopped or deflected by an outside agency.

Sand wedge: A club with a heavy, wide sole that is designed principally to be used in sand traps.

Scotch foursome: Four players divided into two teams, each team playing one ball, each partner hitting alternate shots.

Scrambler: A player who shows exceptional skill around the greens after demonstrating loose play in getting there.

Scratch player: A player who plays consistently around par and has a handicap of zero.

Shanking: Hitting the ball with the neck (hosel) of the club and making it travel in an oblique direction to the right.

Skying: Hitting the ball high in the air but only a short distance, when it was intended to travel much farther.

Slice: A golf shot that curves from left to right.

Sole: The bottom of the clubhead; or the act of resting the bottom of the clubhead on the ground at address.

Square stance: A stance in which a line drawn from the toe of the right foot to the toe of the left foot runs parallel to the line of flight.

Stance: The position of the feet and body when a player addresses the ball.

Summer rules: The regular playing rules of golf that do not allow a player to improve the lie of his ball except under special conditions.

Tee: The wooden or plastic peg on which the ball is placed at the start of a hole; or the area from which a player starts the play of a hole, more correctly called the "teeing ground."

Tee markers: The markers placed on the teeing ground that designate the point from which play of the hole begins.

Through the green: All of the area on the course with the exception of the teeing ground, the green, and any hazard.

Toed shot: A shot that is struck on or near the toe of the club.

Topped shot: A rolling or low-bounding shot that is caused by striking the ball above its center of gravity.

Winter rules: A condition under which the course is not in top playable condition and players are allowed to improve the lie of their balls.

SELECTED REFERENCES AND READINGS

There are over 1,000 books that have been written on how to swing a golf club. Obviously, you can't read them all, and even if you could, many would be a waste of time. Below are some of the good instructional books that have been written. Those that are noninstructional but excellent reading are noted with #.

AULTMAN, DICK, and KEN BOWDEN. 1975. *The methods of golf's Masters.* New York: Coward, McCann & Geoghegan.

BELL, PEGGY KIRK. 1966. *A woman's way to better golf.* New York: E. P. Dutton.

#BROWNING, ROBERT. 1955. *A history of golf.* New York: E. P. Dutton.

CASPER, BILLY. 1966. *Golf shotmaking with Billy Casper.* New York: Doubleday & Co.

COCHRAN, ALASTAIRE, and JOHN STOBBS. 1968. *The search for the perfect swing.* Philadelphia: J. B. Lippincott Co.

DANTE, JOE, and LEN ELLIOTT. 1962. *The four magic moves to winning golf.* New York: McGraw-Hill Book Co.

DOBEREINER, PETER. *The glorious world of golf.* 1973. New York: McGraw-Hill Book Co.

#FORGAN, DAVID R. 1935. *Golf.* In *Fifty years of American golf,* ed. H. B. Martin, frontispiece. New York: Dodd, Mead & Co.

GEIBERGER, AL, with LARRY DENNIS. 1980. *Tempo.* Norwalk, Conn.: Golf Digest.

#GRAFFIS, HERB. 1965. *Esquire's world of golf.* New York: Esquire and Trident Press.

#GRIMSLEY, WILL. 1966. *Golf—its history, people, and events.* Englewood Cliffs, N.J.: Prentice-Hall.

HOGAN, BEN. 1957. *Five lessons—the modern fundamentals of golf.* New York: A. S. Barnes & Co.

JACOBS, JOHN, with KEN BOWDEN. 1972. *Practical golf.* New York: Quadrangle Books.

JONES, ROBERT TYRE (BOBBY). 1966. *Bobby Jones on golf.* Garden City, N.Y.: Doubleday & Co.

MURPHY, MICHAEL. 1972. *Golf in the kingdom.* New York: Dell.

#NATIONAL GOLF FOUNDATION. 1986. *The easy way to learn golf rules.* Jupiter, Fla.: National Golf Foundation.

NICKLAUS, JACK, with KEN BOWDEN. 1974. *Golf my way.* New York: Simon & Schuster.

PALMER, ARNOLD. 1965. *My game and yours.* New York: Simon & Schuster.

PLAYER, GARY. 1966. *Gary Player's golf secrets.* Englewood Cliffs, N.J.: Prentice-Hall.

———. 1967. *Positive golf.* New York: McGraw-Hill Book Co.

#PRICE, CHARLES. 1962. *The American golfer.* New York: Random House.

SHANKLAND, CRAIG, DALE SHANKLAND, DOM LUPO, and ROY BENJAMIN. 1978. *The golfer's stroke saver handbook.* Boston: Little, Brown and Co.

SNEAD, SAM, with DICK AULTMAN. *Golf begins at forty.* 1978. New York: Dial Press.

SUTPHEN, VAN TASSEL. 1901. *The nineteenth hole.* New York: Harper & Row.

TOSKI, BOB, and JIM FLICK, with LARRY DENNIS. 1984. *How to become a complete golfer.* Norwalk, Conn.: Golf Digest.

VENTURI, KEN, with AL BARKOW. 1981. *The Venturi analysis.* New York: Atheneum Press.

#WATSON, TOM, with FRANK HANNIGAN. 1984. *The new rules of golf.* New York: Random House.

WIREN, GARY, and DICK COOP, with LARRY SHEEHAN. 1978. *The new golf mind.* New York: Simon & Schuster.

WIREN, GARY, with DAWSON TAYLOR. 1987. *Golf's common errors and what to do about them.* Chicago: Contemporary Books.

———. 1984. *Super-power golf.* Chicago: Contemporary Books.

WRIGHT, MICKEY. 1962. *Play golf the Wright way.* Garden City, N.Y.: Doubleday & Co.

INDEX

Accessories, 23–24
Ace, 123
Addressing the ball, 38–44, 85, 123
Advice, 82, 85
"Albatross," 124
Alignment of clubface, 27–30
  grip positions and, 34
All-finger grip, 37
Anger, 4
Approach shot, 123
Apron, 123
Arc, clubhead, 62–64
Away, 123

Backswing, getting to the top of, 53–58
Bag
  golf, 22
  impact, 60
  shag, 101
Ball(s), 22–23
  addressing the, 38–44, 85, 123
  best, 123
  changing, 84
  downward blow to, 64
  lifting and cleaning, 86
  lost, 83
  placement of, 41–43
  in play, 83
  playing outside course boundaries of, 84
  provisional, 83, 125
  scooping the, 75

  "topping the," 63, 109–10, 126
  unplayable, 86
Ball line, 30
Beman, Deane, 70
Birdie, 123
Bite, 123
Body conditioning, 5, 103–6
Bogey, 123, 124
Boundaries, playing ball outside, 84
Brands of equipment, 20–21
Break of green, 74, 123
Bridgland, Sir Aynsley, 117
British golf studies, 117
Bunker, 83, 123

Caddy, 123
Callaway system, 123
Carry, 123
Cars, 23–24
  safety concerns in using, 90
Carts, 23–24
Casual water, 82, 123
Centrifugal force, 120
Challenge of golf, 11–13
Chip shot, 74–78, 124
  scientific study of, 118–19
Class instruction, 90
Cleaning the ball, 86
Closed clubface, 124
Closed stance, 124
Clothing, golf, 24

129